TINY DANCER, BIG WORLD

TINY DANCER, BIG WORLD

How to Find Fulfilment from the Inside Out

JANETTE MANRARA

with Lesly Manrara

WILLIAM
COLLINS

—— William Collins
An imprint of HarperCollins*Publishers*
1 London Bridge Street
London SE1 9GF

WilliamCollinsBooks.com

HarperCollins*Publishers*
Macken House, 39/40 Mayor Street Upper
Dublin 1, D01 C9W8, Ireland

First published in Great Britain in 2024 by William Collins

1

A catalogue record for this book is
available from the British Library

ISBN 978-0-00-861922-0

'The Guest House' from *Selected Poems* by Rumi, translation © Coleman
Banks, 1995. Reprinted by permission of Penguin Books Limited.

Best efforts have been made to attribute quotes and concepts; any inadvertent
mistakes or omissions will be gladly rectified in future editions.

Set in Adobe Garamond Pro
Printed and bound in the UK using 100%
renewable electricity at CPI Group (UK) Ltd

This book is dedicated to …

you.

May it be your companion through your thoughts;
may it make you smile, make you question and
bring out the light within you.

CONTENTS

'There is always light.
If only we're brave
enough to see it. If
only we're brave
enough to be it.'

AMANDA GORMAN

WELCOME

Welcome. Welcome to this adventure. If you've picked up this book, you're a curious soul, and curious about your soul; you're intrigued, wanting to dig a little bit deeper, to find out what your own internal rhythm is. Congratulations on taking that first step towards understanding the most wondrous being of all – yourself. To look within is to step into the most intimate adventure. It takes courage to navigate those inner waters, but the self-discovery, acceptance and reflections that await you in these pages are like hidden treasures. Every new twist and turn in your journey will light up parts of you that might have been patiently waiting – longing, almost – to be acknowledged, seen, heard and felt.

We start with the biggest question of all: who are you? What makes you 'you'? What would you like to better, or explore further about yourself? These are questions you may never have asked yourself before but are now ready to start exploring and, at the same time, maybe even finding some answers for. Discovering yourself and what lies within can be quite scary, but it is in this internal dance through the many stages of learning about oneself that we find the essence of what being human is all about; the magical complexities of the 'self', and how beautiful it can feel to fully exist within it.

The self is the ultimate power of the universe. We're all unique beings of light, sharing a bit of our light wherever we go, day by day. We carry our radiant torch, and with every encounter – be it with others or with our own thoughts – we are guided closer to who we really are. If you approach this book with an open heart and an open mind, I've got a hunch it's going to be your trusted companion on the path to becoming the brightest light you can imagine.

Life, however, is not always sunshine and rainbows. There's darkness, too – a shadowy presence that threatens to dim our light. Yet, in the dance between light and dark lies the true beauty of our existence. Without one, the other wouldn't shine as brightly. Without one, the other loses its meaning. Embracing this dance reveals the awe-inspiring nuances of who we are – every shadow, every glimmer contributing to the breathtaking masterpiece that is you.

WHY?

Before we dive into this shared adventure, let me give you a glimpse into the 'why?' behind this book – a little peek into the heartbeat of its creation. This project has been a long time coming, a dream quietly nurtured over the years. And no, it was not a dream fuelled by self-centred glory, a mere statement that said, 'Hey, I wrote a book!' Rather, the idea sprouted from a desire to connect with you through a different lens, one that might be a bit unexpected. This journey into writing has been my way of stepping into a new realm, a medium where words can share stories that resonate, creating bonds beyond our usual encounters. It's about meeting you in a space where perhaps you haven't seen me before, a place where our shared exploration can unfold. I'm not here to boast about writing a book; I'm here to share in a conversation, to connect on a deeper level.

My wish is simple yet profound: to illuminate the light inside you. This book is a vessel for allowing that light to shine, for tapping into the wondrous radiance we carry within. In my heart, I truly believe that goodness resides in every one of us, no matter what our story has been. We just need a gentle reminder, a mirror reflecting our own inherent luminosity, to fully flourish during our limited time here. So, as you flip through these pages, I invite you to embark on this journey with me. Let this be a shared odyssey, a connection between hearts, minds and the untapped reservoirs of brilliance that make us beautifully human. If you are willing to search, you may just discover many of the wonders that already exist within you.

WHO?

First, let me share a little glimpse of my world, filled with the most extraordinary souls who've shaped who I am. At the heart of it all are my parents, Maritza and Luis Manrara, whose journey began long before I came along, yet whose footsteps paved the path for my own journey of self-discovery years later. Their story is one of resilience, courage and unwavering determination – a story that unfolded against the backdrop of a changing world. In 1979, amid the political turmoil of communist Cuba, two families made the bold decision to leave behind the familiar shores of their homeland in search of a brighter future. With little more than dreams in their hearts and hope in their eyes, they embarked on a journey that would ultimately lead them to the vibrant streets of Miami, Florida – a city pulsating with the promise of new beginnings. For my parents' families, Miami was more than just a location on a map; it was a beacon of freedom and opportunity – a place where the sun-kissed beaches and warm embrace of the community offered solace and sanctuary.

Cuba was a beautiful country too, of course, but behind the idyllic, picturesque holiday destination lay the harsh realities of a life under oppressive rule – a life where dreams were often deferred and aspirations remained unfulfilled. But amid these challenges and uncertainties, my parents' and grandparents' unwavering spirits remained undaunted. They forged ahead with resilience and tenacity, determined to carve out a better future for themselves and their family. And it is in their journey that I find my own inspiration – a testament to the power of perseverance and the boundless potential that lies within each of us.

The road to Miami was not straightforward for either of my parents. My father's family was faced with a momentous decision – to leave behind their home in the beach village of Guanabo, Cuba, in exchange for a chance at a new life in Spain. The government's proposal seemed both promising and daunting, offering the allure of a fresh start while demanding the sacrifice of everything they held dear and had come to know. Yet, amid the uncertainty and upheaval, fortune smiled upon them in unexpected ways. As fate would have it, they encountered another family from Guanabo at the airport in Spain, who generously welcomed them into their home with open arms. Together, they weathered the challenges of their new surroundings, finding ingenious ways to make ends meet, such as collecting and selling cardboard boxes to provide for their needs. Through sheer grit and the kindness of others, they eventually secured a small apartment outside Madrid, marking the next chapter in their journey.

Though Madrid was a respite from Communist Cuba, it wasn't the final destination. With the support of the Spanish Catholic Commission of Immigration, my father's family were finally able to obtain the long-awaited plane tickets to the United States of America, where they ultimately settled in Miami, Florida, in 1980. There was one rule my grandparents always insisted on since the very beginning of their journey: that no one was to be left behind. They always stayed together as a family, a trait that was later passed down to me in my own upbringing.

My mother's journey from Cuba reads like a gripping tale straight out of an action-packed film, filled with twists, turns and moments of sheer bravery. Faced with the difficult decision of leaving their homeland, my maternal grandparents made the courageous choice to exchange their home for a chance at life in Costa Rica, entering the same government scheme my father's family was involved with. There, they worked tirelessly in a rice factory, striving to make ends meet in a foreign land. However, destiny had more in store for them. After a few months, a dangerous suggestion led my mother and her family to leave Costa Rica via a system of human trafficking that was smuggling Cubans to the island of Bimini in the Bahamas, one step closer to Miami, which was their ultimate goal as well. They were tightly packed with twenty-eight other passengers into a small jet, and it took them sixteen hours to arrive in Bimini from Costa Rica. However, the real danger came afterwards. At Bimini, my grandparents had a very difficult decision to make. Their hearts heavy with worry, they made the agonising choice to send their children, including my mother and her three siblings, ahead in a speedboat bound for the shores of Miami. Armed with nothing but four quarters and a name scribbled on a piece of paper, the children set sail into the unknown. After a treacherous journey, they made it to the beaches of Florida, and were able to make that life-saving phone call to their family friend whose name was scribbled on that small piece of paper. Alone and vulnerable, they waited on the sun-drenched beach, their young hearts filled with fear. Yet, against all the odds, fate was kind to them, and they were collected and brought to safety. A few days later, my grandparents arrived, completing the journey that had torn them apart. Together, they forged a new beginning in the land of opportunity, where dreams were as boundless as the horizon.

After embarking on two arduous and intricate journeys, guided by nothing but their dreams, each of my parents eventually found themselves nestled in the small town of

Hialeah, Miami. This is where their love story flourished. At the young age of eighteen, my mum found herself expecting me, prompting my parents to exchange vows in an intimate ceremony. With unwavering determination, my mum devoted all her energy to both her work and motherhood, while my father, still in his youth, diligently pursued his high-school education before diving headfirst into the workforce. Their journey was one of survival, marked by the daunting task of learning a new language, adapting to unfamiliar customs and navigating the uncharted waters of parenthood – all at an age when most people are still grappling with life's fundamentals.

Yet, amid the whirlwind of change and uncertainty, my parents courageously and gracefully juggled the myriad challenges that came their way. As my paternal grandfather wisely professed, 'No one gets left behind' – a sentiment that has always resonated deeply within our family. With the unwavering support of our extended family – comprising grandparents, aunts, uncles and siblings – my parents found solace and strength in each other's embrace. It was this profound sense of familial solidarity that provided them with the resilience and fortitude to forge ahead, even in the face of adversity.

As the years passed, our family continued to blossom with the arrival of new life. My aunts and uncles joyously welcomed their own children into the world, and with them came some of my dearest companions – my cousins. Together, we formed an inseparable bond, finding endless adventures in the simplest of things. While our parents toiled away at work, it was our grandmother Iraida who became our guiding light, nurturing us with love and laughter. Growing up in the bustling household of my paternal grandparents, Miguel Angel and Iraida, our home was always alive with activity. Grandma's kitchen was a hub of warmth and delicious aromas, where she lovingly prepared meals for the entire family. After school, we would eagerly return home, gathering with our cousins to play games and await the arrival of our parents. And on Saturday nights, our home transformed into a sanctuary of familial love and togetherness, as aunts, uncles and cousins alike crowded round a dinner table full of laughter.

Six years passed, and then, as if by the wave of a magic wand, my little brother Alejandro made his grand entrance into our lives. We affectionately call him 'Alex', though his friends know him by the playful nickname 'Fizzy'. With his radiant smile, which could light up even the darkest of rooms, he became our family's very own beacon of charisma – a true unicorn in every sense of the word. With his arrival, our cosy family of three blossomed into a lively quartet, brimming with love, laughter and endless adventures.

Of course, life, as it often does, presented its fair share of challenges. There was a time when all four of us – my parents, Alejandro and I – all had to squeeze into a single bedroom in my grandparents house, cocooned in a world of shared stories and dreams amid the comforting chaos. Yet, despite the occasional hardships, our bond only grew stronger. And just when we thought our family couldn't possibly expand any further, fate had another surprise in store. When I was thirteen, my little sister Lesly entered the world – a ray of sunshine with the deepest, kindest soul imaginable. Though thirteen years my junior, she possesses a wisdom and maturity far beyond her years. Lesly is an old soul, and I feel honoured to share the journey of writing this book with her. So there they are. My mother, Maritza; my father, Luis; my brother, Alejandro; my sister, Lesly; and all the grandparents, aunts, uncles and cousins in between. They're going to come up throughout the book, so I thought it best to tell you a little about them now. I'm thankful every day that I have them to turn to, no matter the situation. Family has been and always will be the most important thing in my life. Not everyone is close to their family, and that's okay. But for me, they are my rock, and I love them dearly. There is a famous Spanish saying that goes: '*Lo importante de una familia no es vivir juntos, sino estar unidos.*' Translated, this means, 'The importance of family is not to live together, but rather to always be together.' This echoes throughout my family's story, from the difficult journey to reach the United States, to now living far apart but still being as beautifully close as we ever were. We may be oceans apart, but our hearts share the deepest of bonds, always.

That's my family's personal history in a nutshell. It's the story of my parents and how it all came to be from just two Cuban immigrant families trying to live a full life. Their courage and bravery paved the way for me to be able to follow my dreams, no matter how big or small they were. Their tale is one of bravery, but more importantly, it's a testament to the power of connection and support within a family unit. In an era when conversations about mental health were scarce, it was their emotional fortitude that sustained them through adversity. Reflecting on my upbringing, I realise the profound impact my parents' values and approach to life had on me.

They may not have had all the luxuries money can buy, but they possessed something far more valuable: a commitment to facing challenges head-on, armed with empathy, understanding and unwavering familial bonds. As my father often remarked, 'There's no running away from problems; it's about confronting them with an open heart and the strength of family by your side.' That wisdom resonates deeply within me, serving as a guiding light in my own journey. It's a reminder that well-being and mental health are universal concerns that transcend background or circumstance. Through honest communication, empathy, vulnerability and love, we can navigate life's toughest moments and emerge stronger and more resilient. My family's story is a testament to the enduring power of connection and the resilience of the human spirit. I hope to pass on these same morals and lessons to my own family.

Thinking about my little family fills my heart with warmth and light, evoking a sense of joy that's hard to put into words. Our journey together started with a love story as beautiful as it was unconventional – a tale woven with dance moves and sealed with vows exchanged in three different corners of the globe. Aljaž Škorjanec, my husband, hails from the picturesque town of Ptuj, Slovenia. He's not just the love of my life; he's my confidant, my partner-in-crime and my soulmate. Our romantic journey started in 2011, in the incredible Broadway dance show called *Burn the Floor*, which showcased the prowess of professional ballroom and Latin dancers, many of them holding world championship titles. As we danced across the world, our love story unfolded across continents and cultures. I fell in love with him and his beautiful soul more and more with each wondrous new place we visited. A love story that quite literally took over my world. We were able to travel the world together, dancing on stages everywhere from South Africa to Australia to Japan, before settling down in London in 2013. A few years later, in 2017, our love story reached its pinnacle as we celebrated our union with three enchanting wedding ceremonies held in

London, Slovenia and Miami – a testament to the richness and diversity of our love.

Although our love is beautiful and deeper than I can ever fully explain, in 2023 we discovered the biggest love of all. The most beautiful blessing of our lives happened; we became parents to our daughter, Lyra Rose. She is the most wondrous and magical part of our lives. I look forward to the day when I can share the story of her grandparents with her, and how her mother and father met dancing on stages around the world. I count my blessings every day to have her in my life. She is my truest inspiration, and my biggest motivation to do good in this world.

HOW?

So that is the story of 'who' I am, but 'how' did my career come about, leading me to become an author? You may or may not know me for being a dancer in the sparkly world of *Strictly Come Dancing*, but let me take you on a quick stroll behind the scenes of my career.

Dancing? Well, that I began practically as soon as I could walk. At the tender age of three, I was already putting on shows for my family – performance sparked joy in me even at that early age. I was a pint-sized entertainer from the get-go. Growing up in a Cuban household in Miami meant there was always music and rhythm surrounding me. It was almost as if salsa and cha-cha-cha were beats ingrained in my soul, making up my very DNA. When I hit the age of twelve, my parents saw the need to give me an opportunity to develop this into something more. They chose to enrol me in a musical-theatre programme linked to a Hispanic TV show, and voilà! My journey to the stage and screen kicked off.

Now, it wasn't always easy – balancing school and filming days required some serious juggling skills. Responsibility was my early-life lesson. Fast-forward to me at eighteen, and I ended up taking an unexpected detour into banking and finance at university – because, let's face it, a little pragmatism never hurts. But deep down, dancing was my true love. I knew it, and everyone around me did, too. Hence, to no one's surprise, when I turned twenty-three I leaped into the spotlight by deciding to audition for *So You Think You Can Dance*. Making it to the top eight was a very proud moment for me, but also a life-changing one. It led me to make a major life decision: dance my way into Los Angeles, really try to make it as a dancer, or retreat back home to the safety of banking. Thankfully, the heart won – I chose to dance.

In LA, from the very beginning, life was a rollercoaster. I moved there straight after I finished touring the USA with *So You Think You Can Dance*, with big dreams in my pocket. From dazzling moments such as opening the Oscars to the struggle of counting the days until my cash ran out, I faced many highs and lows. But then along came Jason Gilkison, the director of *Burn the Floor*, and now the creative director of *Strictly*. Auditioning for *Burn the Floor* in New York, I eventually joined the cast in London, travelling the world, making memories and meeting my husband. It's a dance show that has etched itself into my soul and shaped me into the performer I am today. You'll find that *Burn the Floor* comes up many times throughout the book, as do the people I met on it. It truly gave me some of the best memories of my life.

Then came *Strictly Come Dancing*. A chance encounter during *Burn the Floor*'s West End run caught the eyes of the *Strictly* producers. One phone call changed everything – I, alongside Aljaž, was offered a spot on the show in 2013! Eight glorious years followed, filled with dance, joy and unforgettable moments, many of which will also be shared throughout the pages of this book.

But dances evolve, and so did my journey. In 2020, the BBC's *Morning Live* programme beckoned – a taste of hosting excitement. It was this moment that created a snowball effect, kickstarting a different kind of work for me: TV presenting. An opportunity arose, and a door opened into a new chapter of my life. The real game-changer? Landing the hosting role on *Strictly*'s sister show, *It Takes Two*, in 2021. This was a dream come true for me. It was a fresh start, a career shift, but one I embraced with my arms wide open, because, as you'll soon discover, it was a long time in the making.

Throughout all my adventures, one lesson stands tall above the rest: success requires a dance between preparation and opportunity. When it comes to achievements, there's a beautiful connection that happens when you prepare for what you want, a chance is given or an opportunity opens, and you leap into the new possibilities. I once heard the author and podcast host Jay Shetty speak about some advice that was given to him at a young age about how to start working towards something you wish to obtain: 'Knock on all the doors. Not all of them will open, but the ones that do were meant for you.' I'm thankful every day for the doors I was able to walk through and the paths they led me down. I'm filled with gratitude for the opportunities I've been given and for those who believed in me, and I swell with pride at the achievements they have unlocked. The most exciting thing is that it feels as if this is only the beginning. As a self-confessed workaholic, I'm bubbling with excitement to see where the future's rhythm will take me. And I cannot wait to delve a little deeper into the details of how my story and yours can ultimately connect.

THE WORK

Now it's time to pull back the curtain and explain how it was that this book came to be.

Once upon a time, the entire world hit pause, courtesy of a not-so-little something called COVID-19. We're all aware of the challenges that came with it, the chaos and the heartache. Like you, I worried about what would happen if things never went back to 'normal'. It was a time that demanded a different kind of courage – a calmness that couldn't be found at the bottom of a wine bottle. (Although, sometimes, that really helped.)

But it wasn't all doom and gloom. In the midst of all the madness and sadness, there were moments of reprieve, of switching off from the constant negative hum and finding joy in simple things amid the isolation. A little light started to make its way through to me – a new-found awareness blossomed within me. So, I rolled up my sleeves and delved deep into understanding myself, my thoughts and my feelings. The goal? To emerge on the other side of COVID not just intact, but with a deeper understanding of fulfilment and happiness, even if the world as we knew it seemed to crumble.

Enter a near and dear friend of mine, former Pussycat Doll and *Strictly* contestant Ashley Roberts, who suggested an online course, which sparked a major shift in my perspective – 'The Science of Well-Being' with Professor Laurie Santos from Yale University. It was a course of countless revelations. What amazed me most was the realisation that many of the tools and methods discussed in Dr Santos's class were already woven into my life experiences. It was like finding hidden treasures in a familiar landscape, my parents and their approach to life playing a significant role. I enjoyed the course so much. I then took a second course to gain a certification in well-being. Consider me a 'well-being enthusiast'; someone who loves to learn and then share what I have learned with the world. Enter now, this book.

This book is for YOU! Think of me as your tiny guide, your very own Jiminy Cricket on this adventure. (Side note: I'm a massive Disney fan, so expect a sprinkle of Disney magic throughout. I'd apologise, but I'm not at all sorry.) These pages are filled with all the lessons I have learned in my well-being studies, along with some of my own stories and memories. Consider this book a helping hand to nudge you in the right direction on your own well-being journey. I may not have all the answers to life's toughest questions, but what I can share is my experiences, my ups and downs, and a kind of toolkit that I hope you can store and apply to your own story.

There are four pillars that I consider crucial throughout your journey of the self:

WELCOME

I   Acceptance
II   Reflection
III The Work
IV   Discovery

The book is broken down according to these four pillars, for the sake of progression and to help you understand what each of them contains. Within each pillar, you'll find explanations of well-being concepts and tools you can use, alongside some of my own personal stories to help demonstrate them. Use them how you feel is best. It's also important to note that this book is not a chronological tale; it's more like a buffet of thoughts, so feel free to jump between chapters based on what resonates with you, or to revisit sections as and when you need. There is no wrong way to tackle it. I've also added in some of my favourite quotes to serve as reminders of the important takeaways throughout. Let them act as a warm hug, wrapping you up right from the start of each chapter.

I may appear to be just a tiny dancer from Miami, but I've got a big perspective on the world within and around us. I'm beyond honoured that you've chosen to embark on this voyage of self-exploration with me. My deepest hope is that this book touches your soul, reminding you just how beautifully bright your light truly is. There will be moments that feel like magic, and others that feel intimidating. But an adventure is not an adventure without its thrilling moments and hills to climb. And as with any quest, you'll need a companion, which is where I come in. So, let go of all your personal judgements – of yourself and others – open your mind and heart, and let the journey within begin!

PILLAR I
ACCEPTANCE

INTRODUCTION

To initiate any meaningful inner exploration, it's vital that we embrace the reality of things, starting with a whole-hearted acceptance of ourselves. We must be willing to see things for what they are and be able to truly embrace who we are, exactly as we are. Imagine acceptance as a super-power – a force that enables us to fully grasp our uniqueness and appreciate the diverse spectrum of colours that collec-tively shape our being. This form of acceptance is a gateway to liberation and openness, creating the fertile ground where love and joy can bloom. What's remarkable is that this isn't just about self-love; it's also the catalyst for embracing others. Acceptance is about making room to extend that same compassion and understanding to others. It's about recognising the beauty in diversity and celebrating the unique qualities that make each person special. When we accept others without judgement, we foster a sense of connection and unity that transcends boundaries and strengthens our collective existence.

Throughout our lives, every experience we have represents a different aspect of our being – the highs and lows, the triumphs and struggles, the laughter and tears. It's through acceptance that we honour the rich array of our experiences and learn to navigate the complexities of human existence with grace and resilience. As we navigate the twists and turns of life, gratitude becomes our faithful companion, guiding us through our complex journey. Gratitude is like a magic potion that transforms even the most challenging moments into opportunities for growth and self-discovery. It's about finding beauty in the ordinary, joy in the mundane and peace in the chaos. Through the lens of acceptance and gratitude, we gain a deeper understanding of ourselves and others. We learn to embrace the full spectrum of human emotions. It's in this space of complete surrender to acceptance that true healing and transformation occur.

Welcome to the first step of a beautiful adventure. Let's begin the journey by finding out what makes you all that you are, so that we may create space for others to be all that they are. Let's allow ourselves to see all the wonderful things and all the not-so-wonderful things alike, for they led us to the here and now. Choose here and now to learn to love the most magical being of all: you.

'If you don't love
yourself, how the hell
you gonna love
anybody else?'

RUPAUL

FINDING DORY

Entertainment – the world I've found myself operating in – serves as a stage where I aim to create connections and provoke emotion through storytelling. When I was little I was enthralled by the glamour of showbiz – the allure of red carpet events, of having your hair and make-up done, being adorned in stunning outfits, gracing the pages of glossy magazines – these once seemingly unattainable figments of my wildest dreams became my reality. And at the heart of it all, I am a dancer, I get to do my very favourite thing every day. I live a surreal existence that once upon a time I only fantasised about. Which is why gratitude permeates me daily, a constant reminder of the blessings I've enjoyed throughout my journey.

However, beneath the splendour that often accompanies this lifestyle, there's a subtle undercurrent that can often go unnoticed. Behind the glittering facades and decadent presentations, there lies an unspoken yearning for approval, an unrealistic desire for love and acceptance from all.

In the world of showbiz, where one moment you soar and the next you plummet, the quest for acceptance becomes a delicate dance, the pursuit of something elusive, regardless of your artistic endeavour. Yet, this quest for approval and acceptance extends far beyond the world of entertainment. These are things many of us, often unknowingly, are seeking day after day in various areas of our lives. There's an inherent human need to feel accepted. We crave it from our families, friends, high-school peers and even the colleagues we encounter daily. It's a natural instinct, deeply rooted in our communal nature as pack animals. Seeking validation from those around us, we yearn for the reassurance that fulfils us and makes us feel indispensable and wanted. Consequently, our days unfold as a perpetual quest for this approval, extending even to our interactions with strangers.

Smiling at a stranger, for example – a seemingly insignificant gesture – has a transformative power. It embodies the acknowledgement of another person's existence, a silent affirmation that we are ultimately seen. You see, we're all interconnected in this shared pursuit of acceptance, reaching out to the world in the hopes of receiving a smile or a nod of appreciation. It's a reminder that even in a vast sea of strangers, there exists the potential to alter someone's entire day with a simple act of recognition. After all, the essence of acceptance, whether from familiar faces or unfamiliar ones, lies in the profound joy of feeling seen and valued, even if only for a moment.

However, relying on external validation can be tricky. Not every person we encounter will embrace us for who we truly are. This truth becomes evident when we reflect on our own complex journey, acknowledging the unique blend of experiences, triumphs and tribulations that shape our identity. Despite our intimate knowledge of our own story, we still yearn for universal acceptance, even from those who may know very little about us. Think of the illogical aspect of this thought process: we expect complete strangers to fully understand and appreciate the minutiae of our lives – but why? Only we possess a comprehensive insight into our past; the highs and lows, strengths and weaknesses, virtues and flaws. Logically, it becomes implausible to expect strangers to grasp the entirety of our life's tapestry in order to authentically value us.

Picture this scenario: you may come across a glossy magazine spread featuring me in a stylish outfit, with flawless hair and make-up, smiling radiantly. However, what you don't see are the moments before the photoshoot – my initial appearance before the make-over, my mood that day and the journey I had leading to the opportunity. How could anyone, especially a stranger, comprehend these intricate details? And yet we persist in our quest for acceptance, grappling with a fundamental need that precedes all others: the love and acceptance of ourselves.

NOT LOVING YOU

Embarking on the quest for self-love has been a profound journey for me, and one that unfolds every day, particularly within the dynamic landscape of the entertainment industry. Navigating this terrain has posed challenges in reaffirming my own worth. It's a continual process, a daily commitment to recognising that I am enough, and deserving of love and acceptance, primarily from myself. Just as nature is an intricate balance, we, too, are a fusion of strengths and flaws, light and shadow. Embracing this duality is at the core of self-love – a journey that requires us to acknowledge, embrace and integrate both the positive and negative aspects of our being. But, oh, how deceptively simple it sounds on paper. The reality is, of course, far more complicated.

Reflecting on my own experiences, one important moment comes to mind – the time I auditioned for *So You Think You Can Dance*, which was heading into its fourth season. The anticipation was huge, my dreams seemingly within reach. Advancing through each round, I stood on the edge of a life-altering opportunity. Yet, a different script was about to unveil itself. In the heart of Las Vegas, at the final round of auditions, I stood among the hopefuls, waiting for the announcement of the chosen twenty dancers who would grace the mainstage. However, the moment that followed shattered my hopes. The word 'no' echoed through the air, leaving me with a profound sense of rejection. I had come so close, only to be told 'no'.

The weight of unmet expectations settled in. In the aftermath, hundreds of questions flooded my mind – questions that echoed my doubts of my worthiness and adequacy. The rejection mirrored previous experiences in my career, such as not securing scholarships for performing-arts schools in Miami, or when I competed in dance competitions and received low marks. All of which stemmed from having had a different entry into the world of dance. Instead of starting at the age of five in a dance school or programme, as many professional dancers do, I'd performed on television as a child, and I didn't really commence my dance career until I was eighteen. I always felt as if I was a million steps behind the other dancers. Therefore, each setback seemed to add another layer to the challenge of accepting myself and my talents. My thoughts immediately started spiralling. Self-love was drowned out by self-doubt.

At this point, I found myself teetering on the brink of saying goodbye to my passion for performing. Fully submerged in my insecurities, I created a host of false limitations around my identity. I convinced myself that my late start in dancing rendered me not good enough, that my perceived lack of conventional beauty was a hindrance, that my height was an impossible limitation, that even my Latina identity, marked by a subtle accent, was a roadblock. These 'flaws' had become the scapegoats for my perceived failures, casting a shadow over my self-esteem, leaving me in a state of melancholy.

In those moments of self-loathing, my optimism, once my guiding force, struggled to break through the dense fog of negativity. It's curious how, when consumed by such thoughts, the reassurances from well-meaning friends and family fall on deaf ears. No matter how sincerely someone complimented my talent, dismissed my setbacks as temporary or praised my beauty, their words seemed to drift in one ear and out the other. Have you ever found yourself in a situation where positive comments from others feel like mere pleasantries, unable to penetrate the walls of self-doubt that encase you? It's a peculiar phenomenon, the ease with which we discard compliments and readily embrace criticism. A passing comment about a questionable fashion choice we've made might lead us to second-guess our own judgement. Yet compliments on our talents are met with scepticism. The inclination to dismiss praise often arises from a belief that positive feedback is merely an act of politeness. We question the sincerity of the compliment, contending with an internal dialogue that insists, 'Of course I don't look lovely.' This tendency to downplay our strengths and amplify our perceived shortcomings extends beyond the realm of clothing to the broader canvas of life. We habitually assume the worst about ourselves, constructing a distorted self-image steeped in negativity. The damaging narrative we construct becomes a filter through which we view our own existence, clouding our ability to embrace the positive affirmations that others generously offer and truly do see.

Facing the disappointment of not making it through the *So You Think You Can Dance* audition was tough, and getting back on my feet was no easy task. But I firmly believe in embracing the full spectrum of emotions rather than chasing perpetual happiness. Life's punches are inevitable, and like any punch, they sting when they land. The real challenge lies in rediscovering self-love and self-worth to propel ourselves forward. Navigating the labyrinth of our thoughts is difficult, especially when the primary voice we pay attention to is our own. Therefore, transforming our internal dialogue is crucial for emerging from the shadows of negativity. After that first audition, it became evident to me that this shift was needed. The downward spiral of self-loathing was seeping into all parts of my life, demanding a change.

Unfortunately, the art of self-love is not a quick fix; it's a gradual process. No external influence can guide us through this intensely personal journey; it's something we must undertake on our own. This expedition towards acceptance is as unique as each one of us, and consequently the path to reaching that self-love destination varies widely from person to person. In my own experience, I discovered that time is an indispensable ingredient in learning to love oneself. Time heals everything, even when it comes to not loving you.

STORIES OF SELF-LOVE

Before we dive into the next section of this pillar, there's a little detail you should know about me that will make a lot of sense later on: I have a soft spot for the character of Dory from the Disney film *Finding Nemo*. Yes, the forgetful yet charming blue fish who navigates the ocean with unbridled joy. Now, it's not just a random affinity; my sister Lesly lovingly dubbed me 'Dory' due to my own frequent forgetfulness. Despite being nicknamed after what might seem like a flaw, I've come not only to warmly embrace it, but feel comforted by it – much like how Dory embraces her own quirks. She's become my very own Disney spirit animal, a symbol of resilience and joy amid the forgetfulness and any other imperfection I may have. Keeping Dory in mind, let's rewind back to my experience with *So You Think You Can Dance* when my initial audition didn't go as planned.

In the aftermath, despite feeling disheartened, I continued attending dance classes, almost out of sheer habit. Maintaining a routine helped me regain a sense of normality, even though my motivation had dwindled. It was a challenging period, but I persevered, juggling university, work and dance classes. Then flash forward to a year later, when the unexpected unfolded. Jeff Thacker, a key producer from *So You Think You Can Dance*, reached out to me personally. 'Season 5 auditions are in Miami this year. You should give it another shot,' he suggested. Shock and confusion engulfed me – the same show that had rejected me before was now extending the offer of another chance. It was a tantalising opportunity, a door reopening to allow me to chase the grand dream of performing professionally once again. Yet my emotions were as turbulent as a stormy sea. 'I'll think about it,' I replied.

As the conversation went on, Jeff shared some kind words about my talents as a performer, but scepticism still loomed large within me. Past experiences had sown seeds of doubt. Was I truly deserving? Could I endure another potential rejection? The decision was colossal, a crossroads between passion and self-doubt. In these moments, life often mirrors the ebb and flow of the ocean – unpredictable and filled with the unexpected beneath the surface. Much like Dory,

I found myself navigating the currents, torn between the safety of routine and the allure of a risky yet rewarding journey. The question lingered: could I muster the courage to dive back in, embracing the uncertainty and the possibility of another 'no'?

I reached out to my parents, seeking reassurance, and true to form, they offered unwavering support. 'What's the worst that can happen?' they asked. I couldn't help but replay past rejections in my mind, reminders of when I hadn't measured up, when acceptance had seemed elusive. Speaking to some of my closest friends, they echoed my parents, posing the same question: 'Why not? What's the worst that can happen?' Yet, behind their encouraging words lay the daunting prospect of my inadequacy as a performer. I found myself struggling with the decision, as my parents and friends persisted, convinced that not seizing this opportunity might result in a lifetime of regret. The internal debate raged on. Could I bear the possibility of yet another rejection when I had finally swum through the waters of self-doubt and come out the other side? After much contemplation, I adopted the 'why not?' approach. Perhaps fuelled by the belief that it was destined to be another rejection, I entered the audition process with a mix of resignation and determination. I figured that, even if I failed, I could at least silence the persistent voices urging me to try. The audition took place in Miami, as Jeff had said, sparing me the need to travel to another city. I passed the initial round in Miami, advancing on to the next stage in Las Vegas. The Vegas segment spanned a week, with dancers being eliminated daily. I made it through the first day, the second, the third, the fourth and the fifth – finding myself in the final round once again. Déjà vu enveloped me, accompanied by familiar waves of – yes, once again – self-doubt. Anticipating another 'no', I braced myself for the inevitable disappointment. However, to my surprise, I not only progressed to the final round, but secured a spot as one of the top-twenty dancers competing on the TV show! I had become one of the new cast members of Season 5 of *So You Think You Can Dance*! The disbelief was palpable. Immediately, I reached out to my parents, family and friends to share the news. Their unwavering faith in my potential had triumphed. 'Why not?' had turned out to be the right approach. Defying all my self-doubt, everything had fallen into place. This experience cultivated a new-found sense of self-belief within me, setting the stage for a season where I approached each challenge with a dash of hope and genuine excitement. No lofty expectations, just a grateful acknowledgement of being present.

As the series unfolded, I found myself immersed in a whirlwind of dances, each week bringing new challenges and triumphs. With each performance, I grew more confident, fuelled by the encouragement of judges and the support of the audience. What struck me most was the feedback I received from fellow dancers and choreographers – they saw something different in me, something unique. Unlike many of my peers, I hadn't followed the conventional path of formal dance training, but this difference gave me an edge. I was very emotive when I danced, and being in front of the cameras and audience never fazed me, since I was used to performing on TV as a child. That early lesson became my greatest asset on live television; the ability to feel comfortable and natural in front of a camera. My journey was also shaped by aspects of myself that I once considered limitations. My height, often a source of insecurity, became a canvas for creativity in the hands of choreographers who celebrated it and utilised it in routines. Similarly, my identity as a Latina took on a new significance as I became a symbol of inspiration for young dancers like myself. Looking back, I couldn't have imagined the possibilities that lay ahead. As I took each step, I carried with me the understanding that true acceptance begins from within.

Although I felt elated after *So You Think You Can Dance*, a few years later, in the intricate dance of life, I had yet another encounter with self-doubt. It unfolded when I became a cast member of *Burn the Floor*. Joining this league of extraordinary dancers, alongside my best friend Robbie Kmetoni, became a true testament to my ability to adapt, and once again learn to value myself for being exactly who I am.

Our invitations to join the elite cast stemmed from Robbie's victory on *So You Think You Can Dance* in Australia. Joining the cast of *Burn the Floor* was part of Robbie's prize for winning the show, but he needed a dance partner. The directors and choreographers, Jason Gilkison and Peta Roby, saw potential in our unique blend of backgrounds and decided to experiment with pairing us. Neither of us were Latin or ballroom champions, so choreography had to be created from scratch that showcased our strengths. Despite my initial self-doubt, the fusion of jazz, contemporary, ballroom and Latin that Robbie and I brought to the stage became a distinctive moment in the show. It inspired a shift in style, which now remains in the touring show long after our time in it. What had felt like a weakness in comparison to the rest of the cast became our biggest strength.

Like all lessons in life, sometimes it takes more than a few bumps in the road to really learn. This theme of self-love recurred when I entered the world of *Strictly Come Dancing*. This time, however, I approached the challenge with a new-found belief in myself. While acknowledging the difficulty ahead, I recognised that being chosen as a professional dancer on the show indicated that the producers saw something valuable in me. Embracing self-love and acceptance became the cornerstone of my survival strategy. Navigating the challenges of being thrust into the public eye on such a grand scale required a different mindset. Every move was scrutinised, on and off the dance floor, by a TV audience of millions, creating a unique set of obstacles. I decided I needed to change my approach. Instead of allowing the external world to dictate my self-worth, I drew on the lessons of the past – the importance of trusting in my intrinsic value. Thriving on the show demanded not just physical prowess, but an unwavering belief in my own worthiness. In the toughest moments, self-acceptance and self-love emerged as my guiding lights. It wasn't about meeting external expectations, but embracing the fact that however I did in the competition and whatever the internet had to say about it, I was enough.

Life has a way of testing and reinforcing our sense of self-worth. It's a continuous journey of acknowledging our strengths, even when they're disguised as weaknesses, and realising that the very essence of who we are can create something extraordinary.

Just as the unique dance movements Robbie and I introduced to *Burn the Floor* endure, so does the power of self-acceptance that guided me through the intricate steps of *Strictly Come Dancing*. Finding the confidence to enjoy the competition regardless of the outcome was not easy, especially in my first year, but I definitely came out of it with a stronger mindset than I had ever had before.

While the coveted title of *Strictly Come Dancing* champion eluded me, the riches I gained far surpassed the glittering trophy. Bonds forged through our shared experience during the show blossomed into friendships that transcend both time and distance – from fashion designer Julien Macdonald, whose artistry adorned my wedding dress, to *EastEnders* actor Jake Wood and doctor Ranj Singh, whose friendship I still hold close to my heart. In loving and accepting myself, I discovered the capacity to extend boundless love to others, creating a tapestry of cherished memories and enduring connections. Reflecting on my years on the show, I am reminded that true victory lies not in accolades or applause, but in the unwavering belief that, amid life's uncertainties, I AM enough.

BACK TO DORY

It's true, I tend to forget things, hence why the nickname 'Dory' has stuck with such ease, playfully becoming part of my daily interactions, especially now with Aljaž. Sure, it's not always the most convenient part of my personality, and I'm actively working on improving my forgetfulness every day, but here's the thing: when someone calls me 'Dory,' I can't help but smile. Because, yes, it's me, and I've come to embrace every facet of who I am. Finding 'Dory' did not happen overnight. In fact, it's been an ongoing journey, and one I'm aiming to navigate with resilience and, most importantly, self-love.

I hope these personal stories show that, throughout my life, there have been moments when my sense of self-worth was hanging by a thread. Yet, as I've grown, I've realised that those very qualities I perceived as flaws or negatives often turn out to be my greatest strengths. It's about learning to love even the aspects of ourselves that society might label as shortcomings, and if loving them doesn't come easily, it's important to at least learn to accept them and make space for their existence within us. The key takeaway from these anecdotes is this: accepting yourself entirely, with all your quirks and uniqueness, is the gateway to becoming the best version of yourself. I hope sharing aspects of my personal journey may help you identify parallels in your own life, serving as a guide to developing an appreciation for your whole self – regardless of whether you feel those parallels are positive or negative. Embrace these imperfections as the brushstrokes that create the masterpiece that is you – a work in progress that deserves acknowledgement. When you recognise the wonder in being exactly who you are, imperfections and all, an abundance of love not only flows inwards, but also radiates out towards others. It sets off a beautiful cycle of love and acceptance, a contagious energy that can lift those around you. Self-love must be planted within you, nurtured and then shared.

TAKE A MOMENT

Imagine yourself as a lamp in a dark room. You can place it in the centre of the room, but in order for it to illuminate the entire space, the electricity must flow within. Find that inner light within yourself and let it shine brightly for the world to see.

Take a moment now. Reflect on yourself. It might be challenging, especially if you've struggled with self-love, but it's an exercise that promises to reveal your inherent greatness.

Create two lists:

In the first, jot down five things you genuinely love about yourself – anything from your sense of style to your kindness.

In the second, list five things that feel uniquely you, whether you perceive them as good or bad. Maybe you're fiercely opinionated or have a passion for keeping things organised.

Read these lists aloud, absorb them and keep them visible as daily reminders of your uniqueness. Remind yourself that these ten aspects of your personality are better known to you than to anyone else. Your life's journey is yours alone, and it will provide a much truer reflection of your worth than seeking validation from others. Avoid cheating yourself by relying solely on external opinions; go within, explore your depths and uncover the truths that shape your identity. It's a journey that takes time, with its fair share of highs and lows, but the process of finding your own 'Dory' will unfold into a captivating adventure within the vast, unique, beautiful world that is you.

'Whatever you are grateful for multiplies. Gratitude is the great multiplier.'

RHONDA BYRNE

THE GREAT MULTIPLIER

There I was in the heart of July 2023, eagerly awaiting the arrival of our little one, who was due any day. As any soon-to-be parent can attest, I was surrounded by stories about the transformative time that was to come. This was as exciting as it was overwhelming, at times. Everyone spoke about the special moment when you first get to hold your baby against your chest as you feel their little heartbeat beside your own – almost as if each tiny beat is echoing a new-found purpose in your own. During this time of anticipation, I couldn't help but reflect on the beautiful bond I share with my own parents. Longingly, I hoped that my and Aljaž's journey into parenthood would be equally as profound; that we could share something as special as what I had come to know growing up. I was swimming in a sea of emotions. Gratitude enveloped me as I contemplated the precious gift of motherhood awaiting me. A gift that I was aware not everyone received.

That reality reminded me to feel deeply rooted in the act of gratitude every day of my pregnancy. The sheer miracle of conception isn't lost on me. Aljaž and I embarked on a two-year journey, exploring different paths towards parenthood, until the unexpected happened right in the beginning of our IVF process – we conceived naturally. It was a breathtaking twist of fate that left me in awe. Those final days leading up to our baby's arrival were a whirlwind of emotions – excitement and nerves, mixed with a profound sense of life coming full circle. And now, as a mother, I'm bursting with joy, eager to share the magic of our experience with you.

I've heard countless tales of couples who, much like us, found themselves on the less-travelled routes to parenthood. After grappling with the heartache of failed IVF attempts and miscarriages, they found solace in surrendering to the unpredictable dance of life. Aljaž and I experienced this shift first-hand when we decided to relinquish control, accepting that our path might not be a straightforward one. And when, lo and behold, natural conception unfolded in the wake of our surrender, it led me to ponder the invisible forces at play. There's a profound power in letting go of the reins, in embracing uncertainty with open arms. That's precisely what we experienced. It's a beautiful, mystifying phenomenon that begs the question: is there something greater at play, something beyond our comprehension? You may be a sceptic, hesitant to entertain the whims of the universe, but the frequency of these stories ignites a spark of curiosity in me that I find hard to ignore. But before we delve into the realms of cosmic forces, let's ground ourselves in something more tangible, something rooted in the here and now.

WHY BE GRATEFUL?

Creating space for gratitude is like opening a window in a stuffy room, allowing a fresh breeze to swirl in. While the word 'gratitude' is thrown around commonly, it's important to realise that there's a reason for its frequency in our vocabulary, especially when discussing feelings of fulfilment and overall well-being. Gratitude is not merely a fleeting, feel-good emotion – it's the unsung hero of our daily lives, operating in the background like a quiet guardian of our moments of joy. Think about it. Your cosy bed, your morning coffee – these are not just mundane routines, they're gifts we often gloss over in the rush of our daily hustle and bustle. While I'm sure we're all grateful for the roof over our heads, when was the last time you paused mid-sip of your espresso and just for a moment let yourself truly appreciate the taste and the warmth spreading through you? You see, it's not about extravagant gestures; it's about recognising the extraordinary living within the seemingly ordinary.

Because of the nature of our fast-paced lives, gratitude often takes a back seat. Most of us, when we take a moment to actually take stock of our lives, of all we have and all we've achieved, find we are already in the space of gratitude, but it's as if we've put it on silent mode, allowing it to be drowned out by the noise of our daily routine and tasks. Yet, what better time is there than right now to hit that 'unmute' button and let the tune of gratitude serenade our daily lives? Let's address the elephant in the room, the question that arises when we think about gratitude: why bother? Why should we make room for something that we are able to remove from our schedules with such ease? The answer lies in taking action to reap the benefits of it. According to the American Psychological Association, gratitude is not just a response; it's a sense of happiness and thankfulness triggered by a stroke of fortune or a tangible gift.[1] In other words, gratitude is not a passive bystander; it's the star of the show, stepping into the spotlight when something good crosses our path. In simple terms, we get something good, we feel good. Pretty straightforward. Now, the trouble begins when we allow our expectations to soar higher than a superhero in a Marvel film. As society progresses, naturally so do our standards. In a world where technology is working constantly to facilitate an easier life for us, our gratitude often gets lost in the shuffle when we're met with difficulty. What may have once sparked joy now becomes something we have come to expect. Which is why reigniting the flame sparked by gratitude and reclaiming the magic that follows in its wake is so vital.

Life is like a rollercoaster, and sometimes, you find yourself plummeting down into the dips of the lows. It's in those moments that the advice from the classic song plays in our heads, 'Always look on the bright side of life.' It's not just a catchy tune; it's a nugget of wisdom. When you're feeling a bit down, one of the quickest ways to lift your spirits is to shift your focus to the positive. Taking a moment to appreciate something in your life, whether it's the simple joy of sipping a glass of water or the soothing melody of the rain on your window, can be pivotal to your state of mind in the moments that follow. The mere act of acknowledging gratitude has this magical effect, giving an instant mood boost that acts as a shield against stress and anxiety. It isn't just a response when something good happens; it's a proactive approach to maintaining daily fulfilment, which is why we must take action towards it.

Life is full of dynamic movement and adapting our gratitude practice to its changing rhythms is key. We often default to recognising the big wins – our health, home, job – yet the magic lies in acknowledging those small wonders, too. In our ability to take a moment to relish the warm silence of the first moments before everyone else wakes up, the sensation of your feet touching the ground for the first time in the day, or the cascade of water on your skin in the shower. These small, seemingly mundane elements of daily life are the threads that weave the fabric of our existence, and expressing gratitude for them is vital for the universal reward of continued blessings. The acknowledgement of these intimate moments will keep us in a loop of gratitude, thus continuing to give us an abundance of blissful moments.

When the clouds of life gather, my gratitude umbrella automatically opens, sheltering me with thoughts of family – my daughter, husband, parents and siblings. They are my anchor, my constants. The feelings I have for my loved ones are big and significant. But I do not forget the quirky, simple joys, such as my unabashed love for freshly squeezed orange juice. Just one glass has the power to lift my spirits on the toughest days, turning a not-so-great moment into one worth celebrating. Gratitude, you see, is an equal-opportunities emotion – it doesn't discriminate based on scale. Whether it's the colossal embrace of family bonds or the citrusy zing of orange juice, acknowledging and savouring these moments fuels a sense of abundance. Whether your gratitude list is a sonnet or a haiku, the essence remains the same – gratitude can guide us through the labyrinth of emotions. It's not just about what we have, but how we perceive it. So, take a sip of your metaphorical orange juice, and let gratitude paint your life with multiple hues. After all, it's the everyday magic that makes our journey truly extraordinary.

THE MAGIC OF GRATITUDE

Let's dive a little deeper into the enchanting realm of gratitude and the captivating dance it performs with the universe's magic. Humour me, even if you're a bit sceptical; there's a fascinating connection here. Practising gratitude isn't just about feeling warm and fuzzy; it's one of the keys that unlocks the door to well-being. It's like donning a pair of special glasses that reveal the wonders in the seemingly mundane. When we exist in a space of appreciation and care for the things around us, a realisation dawns of the abundance that already graces our lives. Imagine this: you have a specific thought in your mind, and suddenly, you start spotting it everywhere. It's like when you notice a particular number and it then starts popping up in unexpected places. Or maybe you saw a stunning red dress in a shop, and immediately, every store seems to showcase red dresses. Gratitude operates in a similar way. The more we acknowledge and appreciate, the more there is to acknowledge and appreciate. It's a subtle shift in perspective that transforms a little into a lot – almost like magic.

Post-COVID, as the world regained a semblance of 'normality', I found myself seeing things with fresh eyes. What was once taken for granted became a precious gift – the joy of being back at work, reuniting with friends and the hopeful anticipation of parenthood. Amid this return to normality after the unwelcome surprise of a pandemic, I embraced the wild unpredictability of the universe. Work had slowed down after COVID, yet I found contentment by appreciating the jobs that I did have, tackling them with an open heart. As a self-confessed control freak, this was a pivotal moment. COVID shattered my illusion of controlling every facet of my life and career. It taught me that feelings like that were futile, pushing me to be grateful for what I had already achieved. Though initially daunting, this lack of control became a catalyst for change. Gratitude became my guide, leading me to a nuanced blend of control and freedom. The external world remained unpredictable, but within me, I found a world that I could navigate myself with gratitude.

In essence, gratitude became the anchor that steadied me in the face of life's uncertainties, and paradoxically, it set me free. It's not about controlling the external world but negotiating the vast landscape within. This delicate balance, all orchestrated by the subtle magic of gratitude, transformed my worldview. I realised that it's a dance with the universe where gratitude whispers the steps, and abundance gracefully follows.

As the world settled back into its rhythm post-COVID, I found myself enveloped in a spell of gratitude that seemed to work wonders. In spite of the slow pace of my work, I dedicated my focus to the positive aspects of my life, and sure enough, more goodness began to unfold. It was during a work lull that I was unexpectedly offered the opportunity to host *Strictly Come Dancing: It Takes Two*. It was the ideal job for someone who had immersed themselves in the world of dance for eight years, and hosting the show marked a transformative shift from my dance career to presenting, offering financial stability as I hung up my dancing shoes. It was as if acknowledging and appreciating the existing blessings in my life had created a magnetic pull for even more remarkable opportunities. Gratitude, it seemed, had opened the floodgates to an abundance of opportunities beyond my wildest dreams.

Fast-forward a year, into my second series hosting *It Takes Two*, and the magic escalated to a new high. Amid the uncertainties of the COVID era, Aljaž and I decided to try to start a family. In a world filled with unpredictability, we realised there is no perfect time for anything, and our gratitude for what we already had deepened. It was after two years of trying, when we were just embarking on IVF, that we were blessed with a natural pregnancy. It felt like the universe was not only aligning me with my dream job, but also weaving the miracle of new life into my story. Gratitude, it appeared, had a profound way of intertwining the threads of our desires into a beautiful, harmonious design. Reflecting on this interconnectedness, I couldn't help but see a pattern: the more gratitude I welcomed into my life, the more abundant and magical it became. It felt like the universe was on my side, orchestrating a symphony of blessings. As COVID – a time of such uncertainty – evolved into a period of reflection and revelations, I learned to let go of control and surrender to the beauty and gifts surrounding me, both big and small.

TAKE A MOMENT

Try reflecting now on your own COVID journey. Was there something that you had to let go of or relinquish during that time? What lessons did you learn? What did you discover about yourself? We all walked away from COVID changed in some way, and this, in itself, is something to be grateful for. I am thankful for that time for what it allowed me to learn – about myself, and about how gratitude can bring so much into your life.

THE DREAM LIFE

As I hit the milestone of turning forty, I decided to throw myself a big birthday party to remember this important year. For many, the big four-zero can seem daunting, but honestly, I readily embraced it. The fear of ageing didn't cross my mind once; instead, I welcomed this new decade with open arms. To me, each year feels like unwrapping a new layer of myself, my reserves of self-acceptance deepening as time goes by. My birthday has become something of a sacred ritual for me. Every November, I take the time to dive into the well of gratitude and reflect on the chapters of the year gone by. Turning forty only seemed to intensify this practice, as it felt like such a wonderful landmark moment.

The first forty years of my life, with all their ups and downs included, were nothing short of pure magic. Even the tough times, when I felt as if I were being tossed around on the stormiest of seas, played a pivotal role in determining who I would later become. Looking back at those harder moments, gratitude acted as my compass, guiding me through life, making sure I never missed the incredible highs. The challenges I faced were my mentors, shaping me into the person I became. You see, for me, my birthday month of November is so much more than just a phase of the calendar; it's a celebration of life and family, a nod to a fulfilling and still-growing career, and a time of true reflection. November, to me? A time of real magic. Not because of any mystical forces, but because I enter it with a heart brimming with gratitude. The beauty of the world, both within and around me, unfolds like a carefully written melody. Even the shadows hold a certain allure, for they shape the contours of my growth. Magic, in my eyes, isn't a far-fetched dream, but a tangible force we can welcome into our lives, and it all begins with gratitude.

Gratitude reminds us that the notion of a 'dream life' often remains elusive. Without it, we can get caught up in chasing an illusion, forgetting that the real dream life lies in our everyday existence. It's about cherishing the moments, big and small, and expressing thanks for the imperfect, beautiful reality we've crafted for ourselves. There might not be scientific evidence of magic, but, oh, how enchanting it is to feel the universe's subtlety through the rose-coloured glasses of gratitude.

TAKE A MOMENT

Enter the gratitude journal – your trusty sidekick in this journey of learning to accept gratitude into your life. Carve out a mere five minutes in your morning or evening routine to jot down five things you're thankful for. It's an effortless practice that pays dividends in happiness. The beauty of it lies in its simplicity; your gratitude can range from profound appreciation for life itself to the scent of freshly washed pillows. Nothing is too small or too specific. If it makes you feel grateful, jot it down. Kickstarting your day in this way sets the tone for positivity, a little like setting the stage for an encore. Starting with a heart full of positivity tends to attract more of the same throughout the day – a ripple effect of good vibes, if you will. This positivity not only enhances your judgement and decision-making, but also wraps you in a comforting cocoon of calmness amid life's daily chaos. It's not about lowering your expectations, but rather regaining clarity, fostering a profound inner peace that paves the way for a more engaging and accepting inter-action with the world around you. Allow yourself to dive into the magic of gratitude, not just as a quick fix, but as a daily practice that transforms the ordinary into the extraordinary. At the end of the day, in this rollercoaster of life, gratitude is the secret potion that turns the bumps into a joyous ride and the twists into thrilling adventures, merely via the lens through which you choose to perceive them.

For those opting to journal in the evenings, this practice has wonderful benefits for your well-being. The simple act of feeling gratitude declutters the mind, promoting a night of restful sleep. In the symphony of our lives, gratitude plays a soothing tune that echoes through our daily rhythm.

Now, if you're just not the journalling type, that's okay, too! You can still embrace a moment of mindfulness by simply taking a few deep breaths and looking inwards. Inhale the sweet scent of gratitude, and exhale the noise of the day, creating a type of mini meditation, an intimate conversation with your soul. Just a handful of intentional breaths can transform your mindset, whether you choose to do it at the crack of dawn or right before bed. I've woven this practice into my fast-paced life, finding solace in those brief moments of reflection – especially now that I dance to the incredibly fast beat of motherhood and work.

'We win by tenderness. We conquer by forgiveness.'

FREDERICK WILLIAM
ROBERTSON

IT'S ALL CONNECTED

Be kind. Just two words and six little letters – easy, right? It's life's most basic advice, but let's be honest, sometimes being kind feels like trying to untangle headphones after they've been in your pocket – frustratingly difficult. Whether it's extending kindness to our 'enemies', our loved ones or even ourselves, it's not always a walk in the park. It's an act based on intention. We'll slap 'Be kind' on a T-shirt or hashtag it on social media, but when it comes to embodying that kindness, we often fall short. It's like having a gym membership and never actually showing up to work out.

In a world that often seems cutthroat, where survival of the fittest reigns supreme, some may perceive kindness as a vulnerability. So, why bother with it when the world seems hell-bent on an eye-for-an-eye existence? Here's the truth: we are not a species defined solely by our primal instincts. We thrive in communities built on empathy, cooperation and mutual support. It's the collective power of our shared humanity that propels us forward, inspiring growth and transformation in each other's lives. Ultimately, we are not a species that thrives on cutthroat competition; we're at our best when we're united. The simple act of being kind creates ripples of interconnectedness that weave a stronger societal fabric.

Consider the chaos of COVID. At a time when the world teetered on the edge of disarray, we discovered the power of collective kindness. The 'clap for carers' echoed through our neighbourhoods, a symphony of gratitude for the relentless NHS warriors. Strangers cooked meals for one another when restaurants were shutting and supermarkets were turning into battlegrounds. I, for one, scheduled in daily online chats and exercise classes to foster connection and well-being. These gestures, these acts of kindness, weren't just random; they were lifelines. In the face of adversity, our collective kindness became the glue that held us together, illuminating the tunnel with a shared hope. Even while physically apart, we worked together through acts of kindness and survived as a society, together.

BE KIND

Kindness can come in so many different forms. Think of it as a versatile closet, offering an array of styles through which to express itself – whether that's a simple gesture, a financial contribution to charity or the words you choose to say to someone. Merely smiling at someone can change their entire day. But it's not just about being nice; it's about the impact our actions can have on the world around us. The ripple effect of our behaviour can create a wave of positivity. A random act of kindness can be like passing a secret note of joy. You might not see it, but you've potentially altered the entire trajectory of someone's day. And here's where it gets interesting: kindness isn't just a one-way street. When you extend a hand in generosity, it's not just the recipient who benefits – you're in for a treat, too. Consider kindness as a cosmic boomerang; throw it out into the universe, and watch it come back – often with interest. In fact, a 2013 study from Carnegie Mellon University revealed a fascinating connection between kindness and health.[2] Volunteers who dedicated just four hours a week to helping others were found to be 40 per cent less likely to develop high blood pressure. Kindness triggers what psychologists aptly term a 'warm glow' – that inner radiance, the emotional high, which comes from doing good. More than just avoiding negativity, you are actively generating positivity. Have you ever paid attention to someone's facial expressions after they have done something kind for someone else? There's a softness there, and often a smile. Their brains receive more of the happy chemicals when giving or doing something for someone else. It's why addicts usually have a step in their recovery process that requires them to help someone else. It can promote a positive sense of self in them, because we learn more about ourselves and feel better about ourselves through helping others.

In our fast-paced existence, finding hours to dedicate to helping others can be challenging. So, let's get creative. Think of kindness not just as a grand gesture, but as the little acts of daily living. It's the holding open of doors, the smiles exchanged, the genuine inquiries about someone's day. We are, at our core, pack animals designed to work together. Yet our hectic lives can sometimes make it difficult to engage in extensive acts of kindness. I make monthly donations to various causes, and while this might not provide the same immediate 'warm glow' as a hands-on act of kindness, it has its own magic. It's about the simple thought that I've been able to contribute, even if it's just a little, to the betterment of others. The amount doesn't matter; what matters is the impact we make, however small, and the wider effect it has.

Research has found that regardless of how much wealth you have, spending money on others can make you happier than spending money on yourself. In a 2006–2008 Gallup World Poll, conducted in over 136 countries, including 234,917 individuals (50 per cent men, 50 per cent women, with an average age of 38), it was found that 120 countries of the 136 saw a positive correlation between well-being and spending on others versus themselves, regardless of the economic conditions of the country.[3,4] This goes to show how much of a positive effect giving to others can have on our overall happiness levels and well-being, regardless of how much we spend.

Whether it's through actions, words or money, the end result of kindness is always positive. Giving our time and compassion to others is not only beneficial to them, but to ourselves. It can help lower our stress levels, fight depression, elevate our mood and even combat addiction. By choosing to be kind, we help others, whether in big or small ways, to grow and develop alongside us. It's all interconnected.

NOT JUST 'STICKS AND STONES'

As I'm sitting here writing, trying to choose the best words to express the importance of being kind, I find myself thinking of one of the simplest ways we can start to be more gentle with one another … through our words. There's an old saying, 'Sticks and stones may break my bones, but words will never hurt me.' But the words we speak and write do carry a weight, a value; they mean something. It's why, when we share something on social media, we're so quick to read the comments. Unfortunately, even if there are many wonderful comments, our minds have a habit of latching on to those not-so-kind ones. It shows us that how we use words does matter, and how much they can affect us. Words have power, and we must wield them knowingly.

I lost a very dear friend of mine a few years back, and not due to the cruelty of fate, but the cruelty of words. To many, she was just another person in the public eye, but the truth of the matter is that she was a person, a soul like any of us. While some had the gift of knowing her personally like I did, she was judged heavily by the media, who ironically didn't know her at all. Many assumed their words would have no effect on her, as she chose the life of entertainment. Living in the public eye myself, I know that many people assume words to be just words, not 'sticks and stones'. Yet those relentless unkind words directed towards her built and built, eventually leading her to feelings of despair, with the awful ending of her taking her own life. We often make the mistake of assuming we're experts on strangers' lives, when in fact we're clueless about the real struggles going on beneath the surface, hiding behind that seemingly happy Instagram post. My beautiful friend, a well of unrealised potential, left us all wondering what could have been. What more she could have added to the world if we'd only chosen to be kinder.

Suicide is an extremely difficult and complex topic, but it is a relevant one when discussing the scope of kindness and the power of its reach. As we continue to lose people daily to its darkness, we must ask ourselves, is this a reality we want to contribute to personally? How high do suicide rates have to rise, how many loved ones do we have to see affected by it, before we choose to embrace kindness instead? If something so simple as 'be kind' can help save lives, is that not in itself enough?

Unkind words are like little seeds, planted in the soil of our minds. We often downplay their impact, adopting the 'sticks and stones' mantra, as if we all share the same emotional armour. But think about how those unkind words can sprout into weeds and quickly choke the garden of our mental health. One negative comment has the uncanny ability to alter our mood in an instant. It's almost comical how, in the vast field of positive affirmations we may receive, that one negative remark stands out like a lone, stubborn thistle.

Being mindful of both our spoken and written words has the power to shape a society in which growth is not just allowed but celebrated. This would be a place where we inspire each other to be our best selves, always evolving for the greater good of our community. Imagine a world filled with creativity, endless possibilities and a vibrant tapestry of diversity. Kindness is the key to creating this, but it comes with a close companion: forgiveness.

TO ERR IS HUMAN; TO FORGIVE, DIVINE

Forgiveness is the cornerstone of kindness, a transformative force that extends not only to others, but also, perhaps most crucially, to oneself. The weight of resentment, anger and guilt often hinders our ability to genuinely embrace kindness, holding us back. Imagine carrying around these emotional burdens; it would be like attempting to fly a kite with an unwieldy anchor attached – our potential stunted, our progress halted. Forgiveness becomes the liberating act of releasing that anchor, enabling us to soar into the expansive sky of kindness.

Navigating forgiveness is reminiscent of a dance, in which you're learning to twirl with the demons of guilt, shame and resentment. To dance through this successfully, mastering the art of forgiveness, especially towards oneself, is imperative. And like learning a new dance move, it may feel awkward at first, but it's incredibly liberating once perfected.

I recall a pivotal moment in my own life when forgiving myself was the only way I could move forward. And it's something that I feel many can relate to. It was during my transition from dancing to hosting *It Takes Two*. Presenting the show was an opportunity too big and amazing to resist, yet it meant saying goodbye to my daily dance routines. Getting to the gym was now going to have to become part of my life. At first, I was all in, hitting the gym like a champ. But life's curveballs soon had me missing sessions and feeling like a gym flunky. Sound familiar? I beat myself up, thinking I'd never make it a habit. I found myself ensnared in a cycle of personal resentment, a loop of self-reproach, preventing me from returning to the gym. It was a self-defeating narrative – the more I scolded myself for not going, the less inclined I felt to return. It was time to rewrite the script. I needed to stop being the antagonist in my own story and become the forgiving protagonist. It was only when I embraced self-forgiveness that the routine of the gym became second nature (see page 163). Being kind to myself, recognising that life's rhythm includes its off-beat moments, allowed me to smoothly reintegrate into the routine. Life is an ongoing performance, and every time I stumble, forgiveness is my standing ovation. The performance isn't flawless, and neither am I, but kindness, fuelled by forgiveness, is my encore; my opportunity to shine on my own stage.

We all make mistakes, and none of us is designed perfectly. In the grand theatre of life, we all have our share of bloopers, and not a single one of us is strutting around with a perfect script. We fumble our words, trip over our own feet and occasionally deliver performances that unintentionally leave emotional bruises on others. Yet what defines our humanity is not the perfection we lack, but the capacity for empathy and forgiveness that we possess. We learn and grow from our mistakes, and hopefully become better people as a result. Mistakes, though painful, are the unruly pupils in the classroom of life, causing chaos until we learn to rein them in. The key to turning those classroom disruptions into meaningful lessons? Forgiveness. It's not just a gesture; it's an open invitation for everyone involved to learn, grow and become better versions of themselves. Forgiveness, much like kindness, is not a sign of weakness, but a testament to genuine strength. It's the ability to see beyond the immediate obstacle and strive for a greater good. As Alexander Pope wisely quipped, 'To err is human; to forgive, divine.' It's a poetic ode to the transformative power of forgiveness, a force that possesses the divine ability to heal both the forgiver and the forgiven.

I wrote this book with a lot of different thoughts in my mind on how I could possibly be of help to anyone who chose to read it. As I penned the chapters of the book, I envisioned a conversation – a friendly chat over a cup of coffee – sharing life lessons on how to cultivate a happier and more fulfilling existence. Kindness and forgiveness, to me, are of paramount importance in navigating towards a more gratifying, successful life. If only we could infuse a bit more of these virtues into our daily lives, the ripple effect would be profound, not just for us individually, but for our society as a whole.

TAKE A MOMENT

Think about those moments when you've been unkind to yourself – how do you think changing that perspective might change you? Is there something in this moment that you have not faced and may be ready to let go of? Is there a person or a situation you have not been able to forgive? Take a moment to reflect. Remind yourself during this time how freeing and empowering relinquishing that negative emotion could be.

Remember, holding on to that frustration or anger will only hinder YOU, not the person or situation you hold disdain for. Take back control by allowing yourself to forgive. Unshackle yourself from the tight restraints of negative thoughts and the resentment loop that plays on repeat.

A DIFFERENT KIND OF FEAR

When you think of fear, what thoughts and images come to mind? More often than not, they're probably tinged with negativity. Beyond a fear of heights or imaginary monsters lies a deeper, more insidious fear – the fear of the unknown. It's this that fuels unkindness and an unwillingness to forgive, breeding misunderstanding, division and conflict, both within ourselves and in the world around us. At a time when negativity and unkindness seem to dominate the headlines and our social feeds, it's all too easy to succumb to judgement and attack that which we fail to comprehend. This kind of fear has gripped our world tightly. It lurks in the shadows of our insecurities, igniting internal conflicts and eroding the most beautiful aspects of our humanity. It shackles our capacity for empathy and compassion, rendering simple acts of kindness daunting. The fear of rejection, of the unfamiliar, of shame and of pain dictates the course of our day-to-day interactions, both online and off. But fear, as imposing as it may seem, is not invincible. It can be confronted; it can be challenged; it can be conquered.

In the midst of this chaos, there exists a beacon of hope – a pathway paved with kindness and forgiveness. By embracing these positive qualities, we can take ownership of our thoughts and emotions and therefore take action that is open and understanding towards ourselves and others. Going forward, I want you to take this bit of advice from famous author Zig Ziglar whenever fear comes into play in your life. He broke down the word **FEAR** into two acronyms that convey two possible meanings that we can take from it:[5]

Forget
Everything
And
Run

OR ...

Face
Everything
And
Rise

My advice to you is to choose to resonate with the latter. In particular, embrace the essence of the word 'rise'. Consider it a universal anthem, urging us to elevate both ourselves and our society. Picture a scenario where, when faced with a choice between reacting in fear or with kindness, you decide to place the emphasis on the idea of 'rising' in your mind. When the fear of potential hurt lingers, we inadvertently confine ourselves to an invisible cage of resentment. But here's the crucial shift: instead of turning the other way, avoiding those negative thoughts and going on the attack, confront the insecurities that breed fear and try to rise above them. It's a daring dance, but one that will lead to growth and metamorphosis. If encountered with the fear of something that you may not understand, don't merely face your fears; try to transcend them. Deploy the potent combination of kindness and forgiveness, and witness their transformative power for yourself.

TAKE A MOMENT

Let's play with our own acronyms for the word **FEAR**:

Flip
Every
Anxious
Reaction

When you notice yourself reacting to a situation or a person with fear and anxiety, steering you towards an impulse for judgement or unkindness, try switching that response to one of curiosity instead. By letting kindness and forgiveness govern our choices, rather than fear, we can shape a better world within and around us.

Ultimately, it's all connected. Kindness, forgiveness, fear. Pay attention to the words you use. They are not just letters strung together; they're potent spells, uniquely yours to cast. The power of your voice and your actions lies with you. How will you use it? Can you be kinder to yourself and others? Can you begin to forgive yourself or someone else today? How can you rise above a fear that you may have? Where do you see room for growth in your current anxieties? Allow yourself to connect the dots between all these things and watch how you can create a new way of living that is filled with more love, compassion and acceptance for all.

PILLAR II
REFLECTION

INTRODUCTION

Gazing into the mirror is like having a personal heart-to-heart with ourselves every day. Take a second to imagine that moment when you first lock eyes with your reflection in the morning. What surfaces? What thoughts dance through your mind about the person looking back at you? There's a whole story behind those thoughts, a nuanced tale of emotions and experiences. No matter how well we think we know ourselves, the mirror often becomes a mouthpiece for our harshest critics and inner adversaries. In the pages ahead, we will set off on a journey to confront those lurking demons that hinder us from truly flourishing – whether they dwell within us or occasionally manifest in the world around us.

In the process, we'll be diving into the reality of our fast-paced world, which is intricately connected via the sometimes-treacherous realm of social media. These pages will offer a roadmap to help you find your way through this landscape without dimming the radiant light that makes you who you are. And here's a secret to help you on your way: perfection is not the aim. It's within the cracks of imperfection that the true kaleidoscope of our lived experience comes to life. Failure, my friend, only wears that label if we fail to recognise the immense growth it gifts us. As we explore the shadows of our existence in this pillar, vulnerability may knock on our door, and the whisper of fear might linger. But remember this: to combat fear, we must embrace vulnerability. So let the fear in, and face it head-on, with courage.

In the upcoming chapters, we'll unveil the reality of what surfaces when you reflect on the darker corners of your being, and – spoiler alert – those shadows are as much a part of you as the sunshine. It's time to understand our demons, unravel the mystery of their existence and rise above them. It's time to embrace failure and imperfection as strokes of paint that add extra dimensions to your self-portrait.

So, get ready to look deep into the mirror of your soul. I am here to help you see that every facet of yourself, both the light and the dark, contributes to the masterpiece that is you. Let's embark on this exploration together and discover the beauty in vulnerability and the strength to be found in rising above our own shadows.

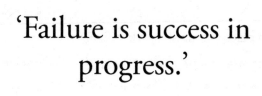

'Failure is success in progress.'

ALBERT EINSTEIN

THE FLIP SIDE

Imagine life as a constant victory parade where everything falls into place seamlessly – where you're always the winner, the star player, the top achiever, whether that means dominating in sports, securing the title of employee of the month, acing a job interview or being top of the class. We often envision a smooth path to success, a path where we hope every step forward feels like a victory dance. But let's be real, life rarely unfolds as a perfectly scripted fairy tale would. Instead, we encounter twists, turns and setbacks that make success feel like a distant dream. You see, marching forward with enthusiasm is the easy part. The challenge arises when reality delivers a swift punch, throwing our plans into disarray. Obstacles seem to multiply, the path gets murkier and our once-crystal-clear dream becomes shrouded in uncertainty, dirtied by life's trials. Motivation dwindles, inspiration eludes us, and the very thought of bouncing back appears impossible. So, how *do* we press on when everything seems to be taking us backwards?

MOVING BACKWARDS

Allow me a moment to share a personal story. Picture me, my very first year on *Strictly Come Dancing* – a dream come true! The anticipation, the excitement – it was electrifying. My celebrity partner, the esteemed British fashion designer Julien MacDonald, and I prepared tirelessly for our cha-cha-cha performance to Madonna's iconic 'Vogue'. As the music started, the spotlight on us, we danced with all our might on a lengthy catwalk. The thrill was palpable. Energies were high and I was filled with pride as he didn't miss a single step. But, as the judges delivered their critiques and scores, that high was swiftly replaced with a reality check. Our technique was dissected, leaving us disheartened. Despite pouring our hearts into the routine, the judges weren't impressed. It stung. Undeterred, we took their feedback on board, hoping for a turnaround the following week. With audience votes now in play, our fate was uncertain. Week after week, we found ourselves on the brink, battling in the dance-off to secure our place. It became a relentless cycle; we faced the pressure for four consecutive weeks until what felt like our inevitable elimination. Leaving the competition was bittersweet – a blend of disappointment and gratitude for the hard work invested.

Taking to the stage of the biggest Saturday-night television show in the United Kingdom marked a new chapter in my life. This journey was my ticket to break into a new country and its audience. Yet, as the weeks unfolded and I found myself in dance-off after dance-off, the repetitive setbacks left me questioning my dancing, my choreography and even my own personality. Was I the problem? I was at a major low. To add to it all, I didn't embark on this new journey alone. It was also Aljaž's first year on *Strictly*, as well as our fellow colleague Kevin Clifton's. The three of us joined the show together. Both of them went on to reach the competition's final that year, with Aljaž and his dance partner Abbey Clancy going on to win the whole series. I was overjoyed for him; he'd worked tirelessly and was so deserving of that glitterball. We were a team then, and remain one to this day, so that was a shared victory. Yet I couldn't shake the feeling of disappointment I felt in my own journey. In the shadow of his success, my loss somehow seemed greater. I hated my mind for even going there. The curtain fell, signalling the end of my *Strictly Come Dancing* experience, and then reality hit hard. Due to my and Julien's time on the show being so brief, I wouldn't be joining the *Strictly* Live Tour that follows the main show. I was disappointed, especially as I didn't know many people in the UK yet, and I wouldn't see Aljaž for five long weeks. Loneliness settled in, and I found myself grappling with feelings of defeat. It was, undoubtedly, one of the most challenging phases of my life.

Failing at what could have been the pinnacle of my career left me questioning my abilities. Motivating myself became an uphill battle, and even the simple act of leaving my flat for a walk felt like a monumental task. Failure had cast its shadow, branding me as 'not good enough' in my own mind. Negative thoughts took root, plunging me into a pit of disconnection. The aftermath of failure is like navigating an abyss. The mind, in self-preservation mode, bombards us with thoughts of inadequacy, urging us to avoid the pain at all costs. We become programmed to steer clear of anything remotely resembling the source of our failure, instinctively guided by the internal warning, 'That did not work. Do NOT do it again.'

THE CAVEWOMAN APPROACH

Back in the early days of humankind's existence, the concept of 'failure' was linked to our primal ancestors' need to hunt for food. Imagine chasing down your prey, investing time and energy in the pursuit, only to come up empty-handed. In those crucial moments, the fear of starvation would loom large, making it abundantly clear that not eating was simply not an option. Our survival instincts kicked in, pushing us to explore alternative approaches to secure sustenance. Failure to secure a meal was a powerful motivator, demanding that we adapt and find another way to survive in the wild and acquire what we needed, when the stakes were high, and mistakes were costly.

Now, let's fast-forward to the present day. While our modern lives have evolved significantly, the primitive cavewoman part of our brain, once finely tuned to the fear of failure, still lingers within us. Although we no longer need to hunt for food, that biological imprint of fear has found a cosy corner in our thought processes. The anxiety associated with potential failure is hardwired, a relic of our ancestors' struggles for survival in a wild environment. Consider this residual cavewoman mentality an old, somewhat outdated software program running in the background of our minds. In our contemporary world, where food can be effortlessly prepared at home or delivered to our doorstep, this fear of failure may seem misplaced. Yet it persists, impacting our decisions and actions in ways we may not even consciously recognise.

But what if we became detectives of our own thought processes, Sherlock Holmes-ing our way through the labyrinth of our minds? By acknowledging and understanding this deeply ingrained fear of failure, we can begin to dismantle its automatic responses. Think of it as upgrading the software, bringing it in line with the realities of our current existence. Instead of dismissing the cavewoman narrative within us outright, let's learn to work with it, to decipher whether a situation truly warrants a primitive response or if there's a lesson to be extracted for our modern-day survival. It's about decoding the messages our brains send us, discerning whether to don the ancient hunter's cloak or embrace the lessons that failure offers, acknowledging that sometimes it is not a dead end, but a stepping stone on the path to progress.

IMPACT BIAS

Consider the concept of impact bias, a psychological pattern that often plays tricks on our minds. Impact bias is our tendency to overestimate the emotional toll of a future event, both in terms of its intensity and duration. It's as if our brains are fortune-tellers predicting how we'll feel about something that hasn't even happened yet. What's intriguing, though, is that this bias seems to favour negative events more than positive ones. We become fixated on the potential adverse outcomes, letting fear take the reins and dictating how we perceive an impending situation.

Imagine, for example, that you are walking into a massive work presentation. Impact bias kicks in and the nerves build, making you believe that it'll be an epic disaster. Your mind starts crafting horror stories about how no one will gain anything from your presentation, your reputation will be forever tarnished or, in the worst-case scenario, you might not even be able to go through with it at all. It's as if your mind is scripting a tragedy, a tale of failure, which may not be rooted in reality. This negative narrative-building is like a pre-emptive defence mechanism, designed to shield us from the imagined fallout of a potential disaster. Picture it as our minds gearing up for battle against an unseen enemy, arming us with fear to ensure we're ready for the worst. It's a bit like the cavewoman days when survival depended on being hyper-aware of potential threats. Impact bias, ingrained in us biologically, acts as an ancient shield against the unknown, a way of preparing us for what might come.

In essence, impact bias sets the stage for failure by amplifying our fears and magnifying the negative emotions associated with a situation. It's a survival tactic from our evolutionary past, and it has found a way to persist in our modern minds. Yet what if we were to challenge this bias and recognise that it's not always a reliable narrator? What if we reframed failure as a path to success rather than a disaster? Oh, the possibilities …

FOCALISM

When negotiating everything life throws at us, it's all too common for us to fixate on the glitches and moments when things take an unexpected nose-dive. It's a human tendency, a little quirk of our brains, known as 'focalism'. Focalism is like zeroing in on a single frame of a movie, disregarding the entire reel of storytelling that led up to that moment. Consider this scenario: you spend a leisurely morning at your favourite coffee shop. The barista hands you your usual coffee, and you sit down and relax, enjoying the warmth and the aroma of your drink and feeling at peace with the world. This pleasurable, mindful moment has set your day on a promising path. Fast-forward half an hour, and you find yourself trapped in bad traffic, your serenity slipping away a little more with each passing minute. In this scenario, it's all too easy to let the frustration of the traffic jam overshadow the joy of that perfect cup of coffee. This phenomenon is not just about savouring the sweetness of a single sip; it's focalism in full throttle. Our minds have this knack for homing in on the negative aspects of our experience, creating a mental zoom lens that captures the undesirable, while the positives fade into the background. Enter impact bias, the stage manager behind the scenes of our emotions, which ensures that the negative takes centre stage, leaving the positives lingering in the wings.

This ancient mental script, a hangover of the survival mechanism that was hardwired into our minds when hunting for our daily sustenance was a matter of life or death, is programmed into our cognitive DNA to prevent us from repeating the same mistakes. But here's where it gets interesting. Just like a movie, our minds have their own narrative quirks. Understanding that focalism is a subtle directorial choice, a mental trick meant to protect us from potential harm, allows us to see beyond the negatives exposed by its spotlight. Like a skilled cinematographer manipulating the lens, we can choose to broaden our focus. Think of it as tuning in to the entire film of life rather than just that single scene. Yes, the traffic was infuriating, but there, playing in the background, was the joyous scene in your favourite coffee shop. Focalism might be the leading actor, but we have the power to rewrite the script.

FLIPPING FAILURE

By facing the fear of failure, you allow yourself to pick your way through the effects of impact bias and focalism. After all, it's fear – the lingering trepidation that creeps in when failure knocks on our door – that often prevents us from exploring new paths and gaining wisdom from our mistakes. However, what if we were to turn failure on its head? What would happen then? Imagine each failure as a primal lesson, harking back to the days of our ancestors. When the hunt went awry, it was not a defeat, but an opportunity to evolve and discover new techniques – a reminder that it was time to adapt their approach. Likewise, try considering your own failure as your companion on the journey of life. Picture it as a guide leading you through uncharted territories, offering valuable insights along the way. Embrace failure not as an adversary but as a mentor, patiently teaching you the intricacies of success. When viewed in this light, failures aren't setbacks; they are stepping stones, paving the way for a deeper understanding of our experiences.

Let's draw some parallels with the dance floor, where my own struggles in the first year on *Strictly* mirrored the challenges of a difficult hunt. It was an emotionally taxing time, and I worried it would cast a shadow over my career. However, in the midst of this darkness, a glimmer of light emerged. A short tour with *Burn the Floor* in Australia became my sanctuary – a return to my 'dancing feet'. The stage became a space of rediscovery and joy. It was a familiar place, a comforting rhythm, which helped me regain my equilibrium. This realignment allowed me to take a moment and reassess the past through kinder eyes.

Recalling the experience Julien and I had, I recognised that even in my perceived failure there were hidden treasures. Through the lens of gratitude, I found a lasting friendship with Julien and I learned invaluable lessons that I would take with me into the future. Gratitude transformed the judges' critiques from a source of self-doubt into the realisation that only Julien and I truly understood our dances' journey. Instead of fixating on the eventual outcome of the competition, I embraced the narrative I brought to the dance floor, finding solace in the strength of storytelling in a world of competitive prowess. Accepting that these revelations would take time to bear fruit, I returned to *Strictly* the following year, partnering with actor Jake Wood. The nerves lingered but, armed with the lessons of the past, I faced the challenge head-on. The result? One of my most triumphant years on the show, crafting a salsa that etched itself into *Strictly*'s history. Reaching the semi-final was a testament to the growth I'd achieved by applying what I'd learned from the previous year. I was proud to have failed previously, for it led me to a better place, right then and there.

WELCOMING FAILURE

Sometimes we do take steps backwards in life, but when we take three steps forward and one step back, we need to remind ourselves that we still took two steps forward and learned something along the way. So don't allow fear to halt your momentum. Flip the script! What if we saw failure as a friend rather than a foe, as a tough-love coach pushing us to grow? Life isn't about the punches it throws at us; it's about how we roll with those punches. We've come a long way from our hunter-gatherer days; we no longer need to chase prey for our survival. We're adaptable creatures, wired to learn and evolve. So trust in the process. Trust that every stumble, every setback, is just another chapter in your story of growth. The next time failure comes knocking, don't slam the door. Invite it in, pour it a cup of tea and listen to what it has to say. Embrace the discomfort, knowing that on the other side lies growth, wisdom and a deeper understanding of yourself. So, chin up, shoulders back and let's dance with failure. Who knows? You might just come out wiser on the other side.

TAKE A MOMENT

In this moment, I want you to open your heart and mind to failure. Think back to the last time your goal felt elusive, that moment when success seemed to dance just out of reach. The likelihood is, your mind's zeroing in on the negative details – classic focalism in action. It's as if our subconscious is donning a cave-woman cape, trying to shield us from potential threats by ramping up our impact bias and stoking our fear. Let's aim to challenge that automatic response. Shift gears with me: instead of getting bogged down by what went wrong, take a moment to zoom out. Can you find a glimmer of positivity in the situation? Maybe a tiny victory or a hidden opportunity for self-discovery? When you find it, choose to uncover that nugget. Now that you are aware of the forces at play with our mind's impact bias, consider giving your goal another shot. It's all about rewiring that instant fear response when failure shows up. Let's decode the subconscious narrative, turning it from a saboteur into an accomplice of growth.

'Comparison is the thief of joy.'

THEODORE ROOSEVELT

THE THIEF

My seventh birthday, which I celebrated as Disney's *The Little Mermaid*'s Ariel, remains a core memory of mine, etched vividly in the corridors of my mind. My parents spared no effort in bringing the magic of the film to life for me, from dying my hair wash-off red to crafting purple seashells for my top – and, of course, we couldn't forget my stunning green tail. I truly believed I was a real-life mermaid princess. Our backyard was transformed into what felt like an aquatic wonderland, complete with kiddy pools my parents had filled with fun beach toys while the soundtrack of the film played in the background. I felt like royalty reigning over my kingdom of cousins and friends. This cherished memory continues to resonate for me, even to the present day. Recently, at the London premiere of the live-action version of *The Little Mermaid*, I shared this experience with Aljaž, and the seven-year-old within me rejoiced in reliving the moment. The familiar narrative, the beloved songs echoing through the theatre, the iconic lines I once repeated to the television – it all flooded me with joy as I revisited that incredible time of innocence. Comparing my feelings as a child to how I felt as an adult – the joy and the happiness – there was a lot of symmetry.

However, the true lesson in comparison revealed itself not long after my mermaid-themed extravaganza, when I attended another friend's birthday that shared the same *Little Mermaid* theme, but with more pools, more decorations, more kids attending – just all round more. Yet I found myself not envious but rather exhilarated by this rival celebration. Rather than feeling a sense of diminishment, I embraced the opportunity to witness an alternative version of the same theme. I was genuinely thrilled for my friend, appreciating the diverse ways in which the same inspiration could be brought to life. Reflecting on this, I recognised the delicate dance between comparison and contentment. In my own celebration, blissfully ignorant of and untainted by external benchmarks, my joy had remained pure and unadulterated. Yet the narrative changes when comparison enters the story – a shift that becomes increasingly pronounced as we move into adulthood. Measuring our joy against the perceived abundance of others is a treacherous path, altering the essence of our experiences and overshadowing the innate beauty that resides within our unique moments.

Fast-forward to many years later. The spotlight of *Strictly Come Dancing* illuminated my path, allowing Aljaž and me to find ourselves dancing in sold-out shows with our own touring spectacle. Each step forward seemed like a triumph, yet amid the applause and accolades, a whisper persisted – a whisper urging for more. We had accomplished so much and still there was this nagging little voice within that nudged at me, saying that it wasn't enough. I wanted bigger venues for our tour. I wanted a bigger flat than the one we were living in. To go on more expensive holidays. I just wanted … more. In the midst of this yearning, I acknowledge the crucial role of gratitude as the first step in stopping this insatiable hunger for more. Pausing to reflect on the wonderful things I already had in my life became a grounding exercise, allowing me to find contentment in the midst of rather lofty ambition. It takes a conscious effort to rein in the relentless pursuit of more, and to discover profound fulfilment in the richness of our existing blessings.

However, there's a sly, more insidious force at play – the subtle undercurrent of social comparison. It can swiftly diminish the brilliance of our personal triumphs, convincing us that our *Little Mermaid* birthday party, as special as it was, pales in comparison to the grander celebrations of life. To paraphrase Theodore Roosevelt, social comparison is the true thief of joy, casting shadows over our unique experiences and encouraging us to perpetually chase after the ever-elusive 'more'.

SOCIAL COMPARISON EXPLAINED

The origins of social comparison date back to 1942 when sociologist Herbert Hiram Hyman put its initial definition down on paper. Hyman's concept revolved around the idea that we evaluate ourselves based on the group of people we choose as benchmarks, thereby forming the foundation of our self-worth and success via comparison with others. Back then, it was your neighbourhood, your colleagues at work and your family members that comprised this social landscape, and this form of social comparison persists today, woven into our daily lives. We step out of our house in the morning, survey our neighbourhood or witness the achievements of our colleagues, and juxtapose them against our own successes. The comparisons extend to our personal lives, as we observe friends and family reaching milestones, such as marriage and children, which may spark an involuntary evaluation of our own life journey. However, often, the lens through which we make these social comparisons tends to be skewed towards the negative, which is why it's important to note that social comparison isn't a one-sided coin; it also has a positive side.

The inclination to believe that others around us are better off than we are harks back to our biological programming from the days when survival depended on the strength of our pack. Examining our surroundings allowed us to thrive and evolve as a species, ingraining in us the motivation to progress for the greater good of our community. Today, measuring ourselves against others also acts as a compass, guiding us to ensure we lead safe and healthy lives. Witnessing someone else's vitality and determination to pursue their life goals can serve as a gentle nudge, prompting us to re-evaluate our own choices. As inherently social creatures, our collective prosperity as a society enhances our individual fulfilment. As with our ancestors, this kind of social comparison isn't merely healthy; it's integral to our progression as a community, fostering a shared sense of purpose and enriching our individual lives along the way.

THE EBBINGHAUS ILLUSION

The secret to fostering a healthy level of social comparison lies in our ability to identify the right reference points. What sets us humans apart from our animal counterparts is our unique cognitive ability of reason. Unlike other creatures, our minds aren't wired for absolutes; instead, we interpret the world via relative reference points, in a mechanism that is finely tuned for swift decision-making in a demanding environment. In the vast theatre of evolution, our ancestors operated in a form of survival mode, where split-second choices could be the difference between life and death. To adapt, our brains developed an intricate system for detecting and assessing reference points, quickly taking in data from our eyes and ears and comparing and contrasting this information, enabling us to make rapid judgements when needed.

However, choosing the wrong reference points can hinder our judgements and mislead us in our thinking. Consider the 'Ebbinghaus illusion', a creation of German psychologist Hermann Ebbinghaus. In this visual riddle, two circles are depicted side by side; one is surrounded by large circles, and

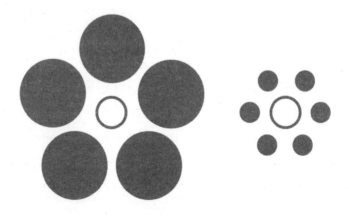

the other by small circles. The two circles in the centre seem to be different sizes at first glance. Most would assert that the right circle appears larger due to the influence of the smaller outer circles. Yet, on closer inspection, a revelation unfolds: the centre circles are in fact identical in size. This optical illusion mirrors the subtle tricks our minds play when we make social comparisons. Just like in the Ebbinghaus illusion, our brains employ different reference points for self-evaluation. The challenge lies in deciphering the true nature of these reference points. In the intricate dance of comparison, understanding what shapes our mental benchmarks becomes pivotal in fostering a balanced and constructive approach to evaluating ourselves and others.

SOCIAL COMPARISON ON A GRAND SCALE

As the landscape of social comparison expands, it no longer confines itself to the familiar faces in our immediate circles. In the digital age, social media catapults us into a global arena, exposing us to the lives, achievements and possessions of countless strangers worldwide. The magnitude of this international comparison is staggering, creating a maze that is impossible to navigate, let alone comprehend. Imagine it as the vast expanse symbolised by the surrounding circles on the left in the Ebbinghaus illusion illustration – comparisons of a seemingly insurmountable scale, which distort our ability to self-evaluate accurately. Social media, a double-edged sword, offers unparalleled avenues for social connection, while also posing intricate challenges for individual management. It serves as a platform where we seek validation but are constantly measuring our lives against those of complete strangers. The quest for approval becomes entangled in metrics such as how many followers and likes you can gain, which then become the marker of our sense of self-worth. Engaging in this virtual realm can be treacherous, leading to a spiral of self-loathing that consumes the mind.

Reflecting on my own experience, particularly during my time on *Strictly Come Dancing*, I experienced the elation of watching my social-media presence grow daily. The public's interest extended beyond the dance floor to encompass my personal story. It was a humbling realisation that my passion for dance had cultivated such a platform as this. However, with the growth of my social-media following, I found myself ensnared in personal social comparisons. Scrolling through the lives of UK celebrities, familiar and unfamiliar alike, as well as global figures, I couldn't escape the clutches of comparison. The initial excitement of my following waned, to be replaced by dissatisfaction with certain aspects of my life – as I mentioned earlier, I began to experience a yearning for greater victories, larger venues and better holidays. I was inadvertently diminishing my own achievements by fixating on the colossal circles around me, just like those in the Ebbinghaus illusion.

The allure of social media often leaves us feeling inadequate or lacking in some way. The curated narratives we encounter on the various platforms, both from others and in our own contributions, predominantly cherry-pick the positive and remarkable moments in our lives. The assumption that others lead flawless lives perpetuates feelings of inadequacy, particularly when our own reality encompasses life's inevitable ups and downs, its tough moments and its dull patches. The constant exposure to seemingly grander, more glamorous lifestyles can erode the joy we find in our own lives and gradually chip away at our self-esteem, leading to feelings of envy, jealousy and frustration. Social media, if not approached with mindfulness and intention, can become a hazardous place. Its potential as a tool for connection, business, inspiration and global awareness should be acknowledged, yet it's crucial to understand that personal validation should not be sought within its confines. True validation comes from within, not from the curated images and stories we encounter online.

THE STOP TECHNIQUE

Recognising the detrimental impact of my prolonged online scrolling on my self-esteem, I reached a pivotal moment of realisation – it was time for a transformative shift. Taking charge of my mental and emotional well-being became paramount, and I saw an opportunity to harness the positive potential of social media. My first step towards this recalibration involved embracing the empowering 'STOP' technique, which has proven instrumental not only in combatting the emotional toll of social comparison, but also in navigating various facets of my emotional landscape.

STOP is an acronym for:

Stop to pause and think for a moment.
Take a breath and reconnect with yourself.
Observe what is happening and what you may be feeling.
Proceed, having reflected on what you are actually feeling.

This simple yet powerful approach allows me to pause amid the scrolling chaos, granting me a moment of reflection on what I'm seeing and feeling. It's a vital tool in understanding the reference points we've been exploring. For instance, I greatly admire Jennifer Lopez, finding inspiration in her remarkable work ethic and life achievements. She's undeniably an incredible woman. However, employing the STOP technique prompts me to recognise the importance of distinguishing my admiration for her from unrealistic comparisons. While J-Lo serves as a beacon of inspiration, expecting my life to mirror hers – given the stark differences in our journeys – would only send my self-esteem and joy plummeting. By pausing to apply the STOP technique, I can appreciate her as an influential role model without imposing unattainable standards on my own personal growth.

SOCIAL MEDIA CLEANSE

A social media cleanse is a powerful tool when navigating the intricate terrain of online comparison. When assessing my digital landscape, I identified several accounts that, upon deeper reflection, left me feeling disheartened and uninspired. They were like subtle thieves of joy, casting shadows over my scrolling experience and sapping the excitement from my daily routine. Applying the STOP technique to assess my emotional response, the solution became clear: I decided to unfollow those accounts that no longer contributed positively to my life. Taking charge of my social media feed, I meticulously curated it so that it consisted solely of accounts that resonated with me, offering inspiration and evoking admiration. I sought content that was focused on well-being, such as motivational quotes that ignited a spark within me, and timelines that related to my passions – dance, interior design, family and the enchanting world of Disney. Through this intentional act of cleansing my virtual space, I liberated my mind from the daily inundation of negativity, creating a more positive and uplifting scrolling experience.

Using social media mindfully allowed me to access a new-found appreciation for its positive potential. After all, while social comparison may be ingrained in our nature, it doesn't have to be a source of perpetual discontent. While we may not be able to control what others share, we do have the power to determine what we allow into our timelines and our minds. This initial act of honesty with myself, acknowledging the impact of certain accounts on my emotions, brought about tangible results in my self-esteem and overall mood. The shift was palpable; daily exposure to content that evoked excitement, inspiration and happiness automatically upon logging in gave me a boost, rather than eroding my confidence in my life choices.

Initiating this process demands courage and self-awareness, but the rewards are transformative. The ripple effect unfolds as you witness your digital landscape transforming into a source of positivity. Social media, once a potential thief of joy, becomes an enriching daily experience. My personal approach to social media has become a testament to this process. I embrace it as a space for fun, health and good vibes, sharing joyful moments, my passions and even the challenges life throws my way. By creating a feed that radiates with the positivity I wish to find elsewhere, I aim to encourage others to recognise the imperfect beauty in every path we carve out and follow.

After all, each of us has a unique story, shaped by individual circumstances and aspirations, triumphs and tribulations. Imagine a world where everyone followed the same script, experienced identical journeys – it would be a place devoid of colour, devoid of inspiration, devoid of growth. Embracing this diversity not only fosters a deeper appreciation of our own journey, but also cultivates genuine joy in witnessing the successes of others.

By understanding our thoughts, recalibrating our reference points and curating our mental diet with nourishing content, we can diminish the power of destructive emotions such as envy and dissatisfaction. In this way, social media, when harnessed mindfully, can become not just a space for connection, but a wonderful tool for personal and collective growth, empowering us to forge meaningful connections, glean insights from others and discover more about ourselves. It's a process of self-awareness and mindful consumption that gradually alleviates the burdens of comparison, paving the way for inner peace and contentment.

TAKE A MOMENT

In this exercise, I invite you to consider your own personal frustrations with social comparison, whether rooted in social media or your relationships with colleagues, friends or family. Choose to break free from a cycle that erodes your personal joy. Take a moment to reflect, pause and understand that the narratives you encounter are part of a diverse tapestry, each thread unique and valuable.

Apply the **STOP** technique.

Stop and think for a moment about this person or situation. Stop your thoughts from spiralling into your immediate response to this particular reference point.

Take a few deep breaths and reconnect with your heart. You can even place your hands over your chest as you take these deep breaths.

Observe how you are feeling and the cause of it. What is it about this situation or person that seems to take away from your own sense of self-worth? Acknowledge your feelings.

Proceed to determine if these feelings are a result of negative social comparison, using incorrect reference points, and acknowledge how, upon reflection, you truly feel about it.

Introducing the STOP technique is a powerful tool to disentangle your mind from the unrealistic reference points fuelling social comparison. This method serves as a compass, providing sharper judgement about how external influences genuinely affect your emotions. By applying the STOP technique, you gain invaluable clarity, enabling you to discern whether negative feelings are rooted in reality. This approach isn't confined to specific aspects of life; it extends to any area requiring reassessment of its impact on your emotional well-being. Embrace the opportunity to STOP, inviting a moment of introspection and truly listening to what your feelings are telling you.

'Have the courage to go first, and then light a fire so your tribe can follow.'

UNKNOWN

BIG BAD WOLF

We're all familiar with the timeless tale of *Little Red Riding Hood* – or, as I knew it in Spanish, '*La Caperucita Roja*', from having my grandmother read it to me as a kid. The story follows a little girl, wrapped in a crimson hood, venturing into a mysterious forest only to be ensnared by a cunning wolf disguised as her grandmother. The narrative takes a dark turn, leaving Little Red Riding Hood and her unsuspecting grandmother in an unfortunate circumstance. It might seem a tad grim for a nursery story, but embedded within it are invaluable lessons about heeding the wisdom of elders, staying true to the right path and the importance of being able to spot imposters. Over the years, there have been variations in the ending of the story, yet the core lessons endure. Tread cautiously and be astute enough to recognise a wolf in sheep's clothing – or in this case, a cunning grandma impersonator. The vivid memories of my grandmother narrating this cautionary tale have followed me into adulthood, helping me recognise the subtleties of life's lessons. It's a story that transcends generations, prompting reflection on our own encounters with the metaphorical big bad wolves in our everyday lives.

IMPOSTER SYNDROME

As grown-ups working through the intricacies of life, we encounter our own monsters, not beasts with ferocious eyes, snouts or pointy teeth, but a subtler, more insidious form that dwells within us. Picture it as a cynical creature residing in the deepest recesses of our being – the internal big bad wolf. This creature, better known as 'imposter syndrome', is a shadow that lurks, casting doubts over our place in the world and threatening our very sense of self.

Imposter syndrome, as defined by clinical psychologists Pauline Rose Clance and Suzanne Imes in 1978, manifests as an anxiety-ridden condition where one fails to internalise success despite evident external achievements.[6] It's that nagging feeling of not deserving our accolades, a persistent doubt that whispers that we are not truly worthy of our success. This phenomenon often stems from insecurities and struggles with self-esteem; it's a little voice in our minds that aims to protect us but paradoxically ensnares us in self-doubt. Imposter syndrome has a way of tainting our victories, preventing us from fully relishing success and obstructing our journey towards even greater things in life. Consider it the silent saboteur, the big bad wolf within, gnawing at the joy derived from our accomplishments. It prompts us to craft excuses for our triumphs, to downplay them, making us question whether we truly merit the good things that unfold in our lives.

When I landed my dream job on *Strictly Come Dancing*, I was ecstatic. A small-town girl from Miami, the daughter of Cuban immigrants, had made it! Yet beneath the surface, doubts crept in. I felt different from the other professional dancers, having never competed or won any titles. Initially, I embraced this distinctiveness, thinking it made me stand out. Little did I know, it was the beginnings of my impending imposter syndrome. Feeling like an outsider is a major trigger for this condition. The nagging thought that you are different, but not in a positive way, can be debilitating. Imagine choreographing dances you've never even performed – like a quickstep – while competing alongside seasoned dancers who have dedicated their lives to the craft. I felt alone, as if I were grappling with unique challenges, torn between gratitude and guilt for my highly coveted position.

I started to experience all the elements of imposter syndrome: a sense of not belonging, feeling the pressure of societal expectations, internalising emotions. Recognising the causes of imposter syndrome can help us to intercept it, but for me, it took time to comprehend the underlying issue. I began concocting excuses for my inclusion in the show, downplaying my achievement instead of celebrating it. When you're dealing with imposter syndrome, you fail to see all of your success, and create reasons why it could not possibly have anything to do with your own hard work or talent. On top of that, you constantly dread exposure as a fraud – you're waiting to be 'found out'. In my case, complicating matters were external big bad wolves online, strangers uttering discouraging words such as, 'She'll never pull it off.' Their doubts amplified the voice in my head, confirming my perceived inadequacy. During this time of my career, the internal imposter had truly seized control.

TYPES OF IMPOSTER SYNDROME

It's worth pointing out, for the sake of context, that I'm referring here to imposter syndrome in a career context, but it can appear in various areas of our lives. It can show up in relationships, friendships or other capacities. First things first, when discussing imposter syndrome, it's important to familiarise yourself with the five known types:[7]

The Perfectionist: This one is pretty self-explanatory. Even if everything goes perfectly in whatever you apply yourself to, you still feel you could have done better. However, this goes further than a simple 'Oh, I could have done better'. This is about achieving great success in many things and yet NEVER feeling like you've achieved it, so that you're constantly chasing perfection and are never satisfied with the outcome.

The Expert: In this type, unless you are an absolute expert at something, you feel like a fraud. You need to know every aspect or detail of a particular thing, but never feel like you achieve that 'expert' status, meaning you are never content with yourself. (This was my form of imposter syndrome.)

The Natural Genius: This type pertains to feeling like an imposter when you feel you are not naturally intelligent or lack the capability to do something. If you attempt something and don't get the hang of it straight away, you feel like you're not competent enough to do it, then or ever.

The Soloist: This is the person who feels as though asking for help is showcasing their incompetence or their inability to do something on their own.

The Superperson: This type tends to be the hardest working of all, and always needs to reach the highest levels of achievement possible; they never feel they are enough even when they do achieve great things.

It's key to note that we can all feel like one of the above sometimes, but it's when these feelings become ingrained in daily life that they manifest as imposter syndrome. This can sometimes prevent you from pursuing things further, and moreover, it takes away the joy of celebrating the wonderful achievements you've made. In knowing the different types of imposter syndrome, you may be able to recognise yourself falling into these patterns of thought sooner. And, in turn, this will hopefully allow you to take the necessary steps to address it and remove it from your life – because you're not an imposter, you're trying your best.

HOW TO COMBAT THE IMPOSTER

The best way to overcome imposter syndrome is to meet it with courage – a quality that has the power to transform our lives. Courage is not the absence of fear, but rather the ability to confront our fears head-on. Picture it as standing at the edge of a vast, unknown forest, with the big bad wolves of doubt and imposter syndrome lurking in the shadows, yet choosing to move forward and pursue your goal despite those fears. To conquer the imposter within us and embrace our full potential, we must summon the courage to take action and to celebrate our victories with unwavering passion. Giving in to the imposter's grip could leave us forever wondering about the greatness we might have achieved had we been brave enough to give it a go, or leave us trapped in a never-ending cycle of self-doubt.

When I decided to return to *Strictly Come Dancing* for my second year, I found it nerve-wracking. I loved the show so much and deeply wanted to be a part of it. But by that point imposter syndrome had really dug its hooks into me. I did, however, have a choice. I could either walk away from this show that made me incredibly happy, or face my fears, ignore my doubts and silence those negative voices inside me and around me, and try again. Luckily, I found the courage to try again. I made the choice to stand tall in the face of uncertainty and embrace the challenge with all the courage I could muster. And oh, how glad I am that I did! My second year on *Strictly Come Dancing* with Jake Wood was a testament to the power of courage – a reminder that even in our darkest moments, there is light to be found if you're brave enough to flip that switch.

There are a few things we can do to help us find the courage to combat imposter syndrome:

Acknowledge it: Recognise the imposter voice within. Realise that it's there and that it has an agenda that does not serve your growth and happiness.

Take a deep breath: Inhale and exhale; allow your breath to calm your spiralling thoughts. Take a second to slow down, recentre and find clarity.

Assess your situation: Are you feeling this way because of your surroundings or what the people around you are saying? Are you internalising your thoughts, or is there someone you can talk to about it? Notice the factors that are influencing you and how you engage with them.

Move forward: As scary as it may feel, have the courage to move forward regardless of what the imposter within you is saying. Take that leap of faith, bet on yourself and rise above the negative narrative. Whatever is waiting for you on the other side can only be better than the current fear-driven reality.

Remember when dealing with imposter syndrome that there are big bad wolves all around us, as well as within us. Tuning in to how someone makes you feel, and learning when to ignore the voices in your head that tell you you're a fraud, will grant you the strength and courage you need to overcome any imposter syndrome.

THE TRIBE

In life, we must grapple not only with the imposter within ourselves, but also with those external wolves that threaten our happiness. The best way to do this is to cultivate your own 'tribe' – a term that has gained in popularity lately, and for good reason. Picture a tribe as a cohesive unit of people, all working harmoniously towards a common goal, each member uplifting the others for the greater good. Your tribe consists of those who not only inspire and support you, but genuinely care about your well-being – those who will stand by your side through thick and thin. For those of us who naturally see the good in people, acknowledging that not everyone has our best interests at heart can be a bitter pill to swallow. And selecting the members of our tribe is not about building impenetrable walls around us or becoming paranoid; it's about recognising, just like Little Red Riding Hood, that there are some people out there who may not genuinely support our happiness and personal growth. It's about paying attention to the often subtle signs of insincerity in others and learning to identify the wolves in sheep's clothing. Forming relationships, especially in challenging environments like the entertainment industry, can be daunting. It's a constant battle to discern what is genuine support and what is mere opportunism. In an industry where praise and criticism can be equally manipulative, maintaining your self-esteem and determination becomes crucial.

I recall moments when the voices of doubt threatened to drown out my own dreams. When I was taking dance classes at the age of twenty, I was surrounded by younger peers and sceptical parents. They didn't understand why someone of my age was bothering with dance. In their eyes, I'd never make it as a dancer because I'd started so late. I was under pressure to abandon my passion. Their lack of understanding could easily have derailed my plans if I had allowed their opinions to hold sway over my own aspirations. Equally disheartening are the fair-weather friends who shower us with praise during our triumphs but vanish at the first sign of difficulty. It's during these challenging times that we discover who is truly going to stand by us no matter what and who genuinely cares for our well-being. Yet, identifying these steadfast allies amid the noise of fleeting acquaintances can be a tricky task, to say the least.

CREATING YOUR TRIBE

Cultivating a tribe is akin to discovering a network of connections that fosters growth, aids problem-solving and propels you towards achieving remarkable feats. After all, as social beings, we thrive when united with others, working together for our mutual benefit. However, identifying the right people for your tribe can be challenging in today's complex social landscape – a challenge that is only amplified by the influence of social media. It's a process that requires patience and an ability to attune to the vibes people exude when you're in their presence. Your instinct is strong; learn to trust it. This innate sense will guide you, helping you to distinguish between those who bring positive energy and those who may not have your best interests at heart. It's not about constructing barriers and shutting people out; rather, it's about discerning other people's energy and the profound impact they might have on your well-being. Think about those individuals who radiate sunshine in human form. Imagine the friend you may not see often, yet when you reunite, it feels as if time has stood still since you last saw them. Consider the person who leaves you feeling invigorated, ready to conquer the world, after spending time with them. These are the folks you want to make space for in your tribe, the ones who contribute positively to your journey.

Often, we fall into the trap of trying to impress the wrong people, expending energy on those who may not genuinely care about our well-being. We chase them, perhaps because of low self-esteem or a simple desire to satisfy our ego; to prove a point that we got what we wanted. But in these scenarios we are always chasing, never being. *Being* ... That's a strong word when it comes to figuring out the kind of people we choose to have around us. Being present and listening to what our heart is telling us about someone – trusting that instinct – will help weed out the wrong kinds of people, allowing more room for the ones who feel like sunshine.

Sorry to bring up the 'C'-word again, but COVID, with its many challenges, also brought many lessons in this regard. Lessons that, at their core, encouraged me, for one, to embrace the art of simply being and listening. Pre-COVID, I was the quintessential social butterfly – flitting from events to rehearsals, basking in the limelight of shows and revelling in a bustling social life. My world was a vibrant mosaic of people and activities, and I thrived on that. Then came the hush of the pandemic. Events vanished, shows ceased and socialising took a different form altogether. Suddenly, the red carpets were rolled up and the crowd of voices in my phone dwindled to a mere murmur. Zoom parties started with a bang, but the attendees soon dwindled. Yet, amid this new normal, there emerged a silver lining – a revelation about the people who truly mattered.

Friday nights became a dance party with friends on Zoom, a lively collaboration with Aljaž to keep spirits high during lockdown. Instagram Live saw my daily exercise classes – a shared effort to stay motivated and spread positivity. As I delved into self-care with wellness courses and meditations, something profound began to unfold: a realisation of the impact people had on my well-being. I was crafting my tribe – one that went beyond blood relations. My family, my unshakeable foundation, remained at the core. My husband, Aljaž, my eternal cheerleader, stood by my side. Yet, scattered across the UK, my chosen family emerged – friends who felt like kindred spirits. Take Robbie Kmetoni: a friend since our first rehearsal of *Burn the Floor* in 2011; now, an integral part of my tribe.

As the world cautiously reopened, the return to big events and bustling social calendars felt different. Empowered and grounded, I navigated the chaos with new-found strength. I remained a social butterfly, but with a profound sense of identity. I knew my tribe, and they knew I had their backs. Together, we became a force of support, encouraging each other to grow into the best versions of ourselves. Life gets busy and distractions abound. But amid the whirlwind, making time for those who lift you up and bring you joy is a stabilising act. It's about listening to your intuition, sensing the energy someone imparts and discerning those big bad wolves from the genuine souls. In the dance of life, surround yourself with those who resonate with your rhythm. Craft a circle that not only fulfils you, but also radiates positive energy, propelling you towards the best version of yourself. It's a journey worth taking – one in which the strength of your tribe becomes a shield against life's uncertainties and a source of unwavering support.

Remember that your tribe works for you, and you work for it. It's a community of shared love, appreciation and inspiration. The same way your tribe supports you, you support the people in your tribe. It's that reciprocity – because you all look out for and support each other – that makes it a tribe. After all, you cannot be part of a tribe if you bring nothing to the table. It's a shared experience that allows you and all the other members to flourish. Being part of it gives you a sense of self, a purpose and a feeling of belonging. So, choose your bandmates wisely and revel in the harmony of true connections.

LIVING COURAGEOUSLY

When armed with a strong tribe and a shift in mindset, those big bad wolves suddenly don't seem so big. All you can see now is the fear that you were brave enough to face.

Banishing the demons is about realising that you are not an imposter, but rather an authentic being. Embrace the truth that those who genuinely care for you see your uniqueness, and want to celebrate it. Equally, allow yourself to celebrate your triumphs alongside them. You have the capability to achieve greatness, and it's essential that you are able to revel in your accomplishments without feeling detached from the experience. This form of self-appreciation is not some out-of-body phenomenon; it's you, displaying your strengths, achieving remarkable feats and recognising that with glee. Think of it as building a fortress against the menacing wolves. Imagine fortifying yourself with a strong support group and a mindset that emboldens rather than stifles you. Those imposters, whether internal or external, can be conquered. Don't let yourself be stopped by anything or anyone, including yourself. Be who you want to be and do the things you want to do, boldly and courageously. Your tribe will be there with you every step of the way, inspiring you and supporting you.

TAKE A MOMENT

Can you think of the people in your life who fill you with joy and uplift you when you see them? Who inspire you to be the best version of yourself? There is an old saying my grandfather always used to repeat to me: 'Tell me who your friends are, and I'll tell you who you are.' What he meant by this was: watch closely who you keep nearby. They are a reflection of who you are. This does not necessarily mean you should only spend time with like-minded people. On the contrary, the more differences of opinion you can invite into your tribe, the more growth can be achieved. What I'm referring to here is intention. Try to find people whose intentions are good, and who have a genuine interest in your well-being. You may already have a few in mind, or you may not. If you don't, start paying attention to how someone makes you feel when you're in their presence, and also to whether or not you feel in your heart you can count on them when times are tough, instead of just when life is good. Those kinds of people are great, too, but often only for the fun times. When it comes to your tribe, search for the ones with a bright light in their soul, who ignite the light that resides in yours.

PILLAR III
THE WORK

INTRODUCTION

Ah, the ever-dreaded 'work' – a word that seems to carry the weight of a thousand tasks and endless chores. It's remarkable how a single syllable can evoke such a sense of obligation and reluctance. When we think of work, it's often in the context of responsibilities looming over us like dark clouds, ready to rain down a torrent of stress and fatigue. It's no wonder we've come to associate it with a feeling of trepidation – merely uttering the word can bring forth a collective sigh of resignation. But let's delve deeper into this association. Why does the prospect of work elicit such a negative response in us? Perhaps it's because we've been conditioned to view it as a necessary evil – a means to an end, rather than an end in itself. After all, when we talk about work, we often use terms such as 'task' and 'effort' to describe it, which carry connotations of struggle and discomfort. It's as if we've resigned ourselves to the idea that work is something to be endured, rather than embraced.

Yet amid this sea of negativity there lies a glimmer of hope: results. Yes, buried within the definition of work lies the promise of results – outcomes that signify progress, growth and achievement. It's through our efforts that we not only develop and adapt, but also uncover new opportunities and avenues to pursue. In fact, if we dare to redefine 'work' through the lens of 'results', suddenly the concept takes on a whole new light. Instead of dreading it, we can begin to see it as a journey towards something meaningful, a path paved with possibilities. So, while work may not always sound like the most enticing prospect, let's not forget its potential to lead us towards remarkable results. After all, isn't it the pursuit of those very outcomes that makes the journey worthwhile? Let's embrace the challenge of work, knowing that with every bit of effort we expend, we inch closer to the transformative power of progress.

Choosing to work on ourselves is one of the most important things we can do. Embarking on the journey of self-discovery is a profoundly enriching experience that transcends mere introspection; it's a testament to our commitment to personal growth and enlightenment. Within each of us lies the potential for profound transformation and a deeper understanding of our true self. However, like any significant undertaking, this journey requires dedication, perseverance and a willingness to delve into the depths of our being. The road to self-development is not always straightforward; it's marked by challenges, obstacles and moments of introspection that demand our attention and effort. Yet it's through facing these challenges that we cultivate resilience, strength and a deeper sense of self-awareness. Each step we take on this journey brings us closer to unlocking our full potential and realising the innate wisdom that resides within us.

Moreover, the rewards of self-discovery extend far beyond the mere act of introspection. There's a profound sense of satisfaction that comes from overcoming hurdles, pushing past our limits and witnessing our own growth. It's in those moments of struggle and perseverance that we truly come to appreciate the beauty and life-changing effects of the journey we've been on.

In essence, the work of self-discovery is a multifaceted endeavour that includes both inner reflection and outward action. It requires us to confront our fears, embrace our vulnerabilities and strive for authenticity in every aspect of our lives. And while the way may be hard-going at times, the rewards – the profound sense of fulfilment, the deep connection to our true selves and the boundless potential for evolution – are immeasurable. So, let us embark on this journey with courage, determination and an unwavering commitment to personal growth. Let us embrace the challenges that lie ahead as opportunities for change. For in the pursuit of self-discovery, we not only uncover our true essence, but also lay the foundation for a life of meaning and satisfaction.

Equipping ourselves with the essential tools for this inner workshop is not just advantageous – it's imperative. These tools serve as our trusted companions, guiding us through the intricate process of doing the work on ourselves. They will steer us through the toughest of moments, offering solace and direction when the path ahead seems uncertain. In moments of weakness, they become our source of strength, empowering us to persevere in the face of adversity. Like steadfast allies, they will stand by our side in the battles we'll encounter along the way, arming us with the resilience and determination we need to overcome any obstacle.

These tools are more than just instruments; they are beacons of light illuminating the darkest corners of our journey. In times of doubt and despair, they serve as our guide, leading us towards the realisation of our true potential. They provide stability amid the twists and turns that characterise the road to self-discovery. And if we have the courage and vulnerability to allow them to lead us, we will yield unimaginable results – revealing the beauty and brilliance that lies within each of us. So, let us embrace what lies ahead, knowing that with the right tools at our disposal, we can achieve extraordinary outcomes.

'You can, you should, and if you're brave enough to start, you will.'

STEPHEN KING

WHERE TO START?

'THE SKY'S THE LIMIT!' 'FOLLOW YOUR DREAMS!' 'YOU CAN DO THIS!' Sounds familiar, right? It's not uncommon to read a headline cheering us on to create a shift in our lives – and while I love what the big, beautiful words above embody, we're seldom taught the big, beautiful changes that need to take place in order to actualise them. We all have the capacity to achieve anything we set our minds to, but the 'achieving' bit lies entirely in the act of us *doing*. That's where it can get tricky. Finding the momentum within ourselves to do the work and put the change in motion, especially when we're feeling particularly stagnant, can feel almost impossible. Sometimes, just the mere thought of starting something is enough to blow out the spark that ignited the desire for change to begin with. So, we avoid it. When we're feeling overwhelmed or underqualified it can become a knee-jerk reaction for us to put the thoughts that are causing the uneasiness behind us, in the belief that we will deal with them another day. This pattern can be dangerous. If you put off the work today, you can do so again tomorrow, and then what's to stop you from doing it again the day after that? Before you know it weeks, months and even years can go by, and there you remain, stuck.

I've seen this happen often – not only to the people around me, but countless times in my own life. Times when I felt truly stuck, without a way out. It was in those low-frequency moments that doubt really made itself known, emerging as if fully formed from the shadows of my own fear. I doubted that I had any talent. I doubted that I could make it in the world of entertainment. More recently, I doubted that I would be able to transition from being known as a dancer to being a TV presenter. You see, doubt is persistent. Even when you achieve what your doubt has labelled as 'impossible', proving it wrong, it simply shifts its focus to the next thing you think you can't do. So, if doubt has managed to back you into a corner, it's important to note that you are now in the best place to begin observing your thoughts. Rather than choosing what feels safe or comfortable, we *can* choose to deviate from our usual path, and, as uncomfortable as that feels, this is where the act of doing takes its first steps.

Naturally, the first thing we ask ourselves when we want to create change is, 'Where do I start?' Which is a fair question. Before you can begin to make any external changes in your life, big or small, you must first address what's going on for you inside. What I mean by this is that any form of action requires thought. You need to be aware that you want to read a book in order to pick one up and open it. Similarly, in order to understand our thoughts, we have to actively look within to find them and assess them. A simple but often overlooked step comes first ... a deep breath.

LISTENING WITHIN

Breathing is something we do with little to no thought or effort. So much so that we seem to forget its intrinsic value to the self. When we find ourselves overstimulated by the day-to-day, choosing to focus on deep breaths can be both grounding and illuminating. When you allow yourself a moment to sit and really feel each inhale and exhale make its way through your body, you start to sit more fully within yourself. Then you'll begin to take notice of a little voice inside your head. This voice is your guide, your very own Jiminy Cricket, if you will. From a place deep within you, this voice pilots you through life. And in those moments when you allow yourself to be fully engulfed by the rhythmic flow of your breathing, you will find that this little guiding voice inside your head isn't so little at all. In fact, with each breath you can hear it speak your truths with greater candour and confidence, urging you to follow it towards what truly brings you joy. But this inner voice can only be heard if you allow yourself the space and time to listen.

Gradually, you'll notice that the more you pay attention to this inner voice, the more attention it pays to you; the stronger it gets and the stronger you feel. However, that doesn't mean the path will be straightforward or quick. From a young age, some people are born knowing exactly what they aspire to in life, while for others it takes years of trial and error to gain a true sense of what makes them happy. At age thirty, Harrison Ford was a carpenter, but by thirty-five he was Hans Solo in *Star Wars*. This is not meant to negate the value and importance of his life prior to his major acting debut, but instead to offer a sense of perspective, and to show that finding the answers sometimes takes time – a long time. If you're at a crossroads in life, you don't necessarily need an immediate answer, and chances are you won't get one, but what you do need is a nudge in the right direction, or any direction at all for that matter. Momentum, that's what we should be seeking. I have found that breathing mindfully for just a few minutes every day has been the most consistent and gentle nudge towards action in my life, and I urge you to welcome it into yours.

As you continue to breathe and draw the inner voice to the forefront of your mind, you will eventually begin to feel a sense of calm. This calm often leads to clarity of thought. These are the thoughts we want to tune in to. Listen to them attentively. What is the voice trying to communicate to you? Sit with that as long as you need.

A STORY OF BEGINNINGS

I have experienced a time in my life when I was desperately seeking clarity. Truth be told, I felt lost. But I found that whenever I closed my eyes, took a deep breath and listened within, I was always transported to the same core memories: dancing and my family. Here's the story of how I tuned in to those memories and the feelings they evoked, and changed the course of my life …

If there's something you should know about twelve-year-old Janette, it's that she loved to perform. Our family constantly had big parties; every weekend there was something or someone to celebrate. I remember I would put on shows at these parties, in which my cousins and I each had lines and a role to play. I had so much fun, and this was what made my mum take notice and think to herself, 'She loves dancing and performing for us here at home; why not expand that to a real stage so she can really perform?'

Just as *Strictly Come Dancing* is a Saturday-night staple in the United Kingdom, for Spanish-speaking channels in America, there was a hugely popular show called *Sábado Gigante*. Directly translated, it means 'Giant Saturday'. It was a variety show that ran for hours every Saturday evening. In fact, it holds the Guinness World Record for the longest-running TV variety show, broadcasting for fifty-three years and forty-two days without a single rerun, as well as the world record for the longest-running variety TV show hosted by the same presenter, Don Francisco. It was such a fun show. It included all sorts of games, comedy skits, audience participation, celebrity guests, and even a cast of kids who would perform weekly, dancing and singing. This was where I came in.

I eagerly auditioned, though not thinking too much of it, and actually landed a role as part of the core cast of kids on the show, kickstarting my television career at the age of twelve. One of the producers of the programme also owned a musical theatre school. It was way beyond the financial scope of possibility for my family at the time to send me there, but the owner of the school believed in me. She offered my parents an incredible deal, one that allowed my dream of attending to become a reality. For one hour, five days a week, I would alternate between acting, dancing and singing courses. It may not have appeared like much to most, but to me it meant the world.

Gosh, waking up on studio recording days was my favourite, though. The buzz of being on set with the host, the celebrity guests and the friends I'd made from the cast – it all fuelled me with an energy unlike any other. I was in my element. I was in my happy place. I remained on the show for several years – all the way up until high school I was performing weekly – but as I came to learn, time really *does* fly when you're having fun. Before I knew it, it was my eighteenth birthday. Things began to move quickly after that. I was graduating high school and all that was on my mind was that I was no longer a kid. My time on *Sábado Gigante* had reached its natural end. Now what? I could sing, act and dance, but I also had no idea how to capitalise on that. You weren't necessarily going to find West End and Broadway shows in Miami, and I didn't have the money to move to either of those places. My parents had both my brother and sister to look after as well, and yet they never once asked me to contribute any money for the upkeep of the house, instead always gladly offering me whatever they could. They had the magic ability of making even a little feel like a lot. Asking them for the money to fund a move was out of the question. So, I could choose to sit and dwell on my situation, but the reality was I couldn't do that for very long: I needed a job. It was time I began to live with a degree of autonomy, not just for me, but also for my parents.

And so, at eighteen years old and fresh out of high school, a new era began for me as I fully embraced the whirlwind that is adulthood. This was a time filled with change and lots of big firsts for me. All the while, I was fully supporting myself: I got my first apartment and my very own car. I even had my first real big-girl job, working at a bank from Monday to Friday – a proper nine-to-five. Simultaneously, I was also attending university where I ended up choosing to study finance. I'd always had a knack for numbers, and landing the job at the bank felt like a natural progression. Growing up, I was always aware of how expensive going to university would be. I knew my only chance of pursuing an education past high school would depend on me financing it myself, and this made me highly studious from a young age. Through hard work, I ended up graduating high school at the top of my class. This earned me a full scholarship to any university within the state of Florida. Thinking of that Janette now, I can't help but wonder how different my life could have been. Even though this wasn't the path I ended up pursuing, I always look back on this time proudly. I enjoyed learning more at my banking job every day and, ultimately, I felt accomplished, as though I were on a great trajectory towards a successful career. So much of who I am today was forged during those years.

But even then, in the midst of an impossibly busy schedule, I kept dancing – as a hobby and as something I did just for me. After a long day of both work and school, I would make my way to an empty dance room, as I was often too late for a proper class – I didn't care; anything to get me moving. No matter how tired I was, I was never too tired to dance. I yearned to do more of it. I longed to make dance my full-time career, but how could I ever take something so uncertain seriously? Yes, it made me happier than anything else did, but no matter how much the little voice in my head shouted, 'This is what I love to do!' I couldn't shake the reality of life and the bills that came with it. Internally, this was a very conflicting time for me. Professionally and academically, I found myself aligned with a traditional route to success, one where I was rapidly seeing growth and results as I moved up the banking ladder. A route that offered me the financial stability I didn't have in my life growing up. A route I liked and found interesting, and also happened to be skilled at. For quite some time, I found myself stuck in the hamster wheel of life. I listened to the inner critic as it told me dancing was not a sustainable or plausible career choice and that it could only ever be a hobby. I listened as it told me that it was time to grow up and grab the opportunities before me and finally let go of my dancing dream. For that was all it was good for … dreaming.

I excelled in my banking career as I continued to do well in the company, and it was only as others continually cele-brated me that I realised how wrong the 'right' path could feel if your heart wasn't in it. Bottom line: I wasn't happy, and I wasn't feeling fulfilled in my life. Something needed to change. It was in the midst of this confusing time that I made some much-needed room for stillness and I finally took a long-overdue deep breath. I intentionally sought out the voice within me and finally it hit me. Clarity. I felt the purest thoughts arise as I was transported back to when I was a kid putting on performances at family parties. I heard the laughter within the salsa music; I saw my mum's smile as she recorded me dancing with my dad; I remembered how I felt performing on *Sábado Gigante*, and as the memories continued to flash before me, intense feelings of warmth and happiness began to engulf me from head to toe. And then it dawned on me: dancing equated to joy.

Whenever I danced I felt as if I transcended the mundanity of the everyday and morphed into my purest form. I *became* the instruments I heard, letting the music live and breathe through me, as if demanding to tell a story only my movements could convey. Goosebumps would take over my skin. It was the closest thing I ever felt to real magic. A feeling too beautiful and too deep for me to ever find the right words to describe, and this made something abundantly clear to me. I didn't want to dance, I didn't like to dance, I *needed* to dance. And so … I danced.

Life has a way of making cynics out of us. In many ways, we sometimes become too 'adult' and stop tuning in to what the little voice within us doesn't just want, but often needs. For me, that was dance, but it can be an infinite number of possibilities for you. Writing, photography, maths, science, literature, teaching, animation, being of service; anything, so long as it engages your joy and curiosity. Ultimately, whether we're discussing work or our personal lives, we all desperately long to spend our time doing things that make us feel fulfilled. There's a reason why the saying 'If you love what you do, you'll never work a day in your life' is so commonly used. It's beyond valuable to make a note of activities and moments that bring you joy. It may not necessarily be something you wish to make a career out of, but it could be something you can incorporate more into your life to elevate your feelings of joy. At the other end of the spectrum, perhaps there is something you can do less of to create more space for feelings of joy.

TAKE A MOMENT

Find a moment right now to get comfortable and take a nice, long, deep breath in. Just listen. Be mindful. What comes up? What feelings are arising from those continued deep breaths? What voice is screaming the loudest to be heard? Is there something you want to change in your life?

Once that internal desire has made itself known and you've experienced clarity, what comes next? We now know what we want or what we'd actively like to seek out more, but how can we apply ourselves to making this happen in daily life and move towards achieving it? Well, this is where I WOOP and cheer loudly … quite literally.

WOOP

WOOP is a form of visualisation created by psychologist and researcher Gabriele Oettingen.[8] The word WOOP is an acronym for:

Wish
Outcome
Obstacle
Plan

The basic thought behind this exercise is to envision your *wish*, or what you want to achieve, imagine what the *outcome* would be if it became a reality, and then do the same for how you would feel if there was an *obstacle* to realising this wish and it did not come true. By creating this opposition of thought, also known as 'mental contrasting', you enable a response within you where your body can feel the negative impact that not fulfilling your wish would have upon you, making you want to pursue your wish more actively.

For the *plan* aspect, you would then take steps to actualise your wish using something called 'intentional implementation'. This simply means using the words 'if' and 'then' to figure out mindfully and purposefully what the various outcomes of implementing your plan could be. For example, '*If* I go to the gym today, *then* I'll feel really good and start getting into shape.' Or, 'If I don't quit smoking, *then* I may be putting my body in serious danger.'

Have you ever realised how much something was worth to you only after you'd lost it? Unfortunately, it's impossible to go back and change the past. Fortunately, however, using a technique such as WOOP will encourage you to take notice of the value a wish has in your life without you having to lose it. It helps you explore the positive and negative feelings of something whether it is happening or not. This is why WOOP is such a useful emotional visualisation technique, which, once applied, can nudge you forwards into taking action.

TAKE A MOMENT

Let's break down WOOP and dive further into how it's used by applying it to my own dream of becoming a dancer.

Wish: After taking the time to breathe and really listen within, I realised that my wish was to become a dancer and find a way to make money to support myself doing so. I wanted to work in television and perform on stages across the globe.

Outcome: This would result in me feeling ultimate happiness, while at the same time being financially stable. I would be working, but also doing what I loved.

Obstacle: Time. I had a full-time job at the bank that I could not quit for financial reasons, and I needed to continue attending my university courses. There was very little time in the week to make it work.

Plan: *If* I did not find the time, *then* I would have to end my dream of dancing professionally. *If* I could condense my university courses to two or three classes a week, *then* I would create more time to attend dance classes after work.

As I began implementing the changes above, before I knew it, I was dancing three to four days a week, going to university on the other days, and still managing to work my full-time hours at the bank. My dancing was getting better and opportunities that would one day lead to my professional dance career were in motion. Was I tired? Absolutely, but I had been tired before the switch in my schedule. The fundamental difference now was that I was tired but fulfilled, knowing I was actively working towards something that could make me very happy. I was fortunate that, in time, my dance career took off, but I always thought to myself that even if it hadn't, I was happier then than I had been before. By allowing myself to make time for the thing I loved, I'd made room for more joy in my life. Here's the thing about scheduling something you genuinely love into your routine: it can never make your day worse. It can only ever make it better.

Needless to say, life is a rollercoaster of experiences and we'll constantly have to adjust our approach to best manoeuvre around the unexpected obstacles. Allow yourself to lean on the WOOP technique, work with it and make necessary adjustments; don't merely count on it to be the solution. Befriend it and continue to show up for your goal, just as you want it to one day show up for you. While it's not there to be a quick fix for everything, ultimately, little by little, WOOP can take you one cha-cha-cha step closer to what you'd like to achieve.

DREAMS COME TRUE THROUGH WORK

Life really is like a pendulum, operating in a series of lows and highs, and just when you think you've cracked the code, the universe throws in another number for you to decipher. It's in these moments that a directional shift you didn't expect takes place, and that's when having a tool like WOOP in your pocket can prove useful. You may not be able to dodge the curve balls, but it sure can help quicken the speed at which you work around them. The truth is, there's no secret solution or one way to make everything always work out, but there's something really special about choosing something continuously, sticking with your goal even when it's something far away. Choosing to adapt and make yourself malleable is a valuable intentional act, because you've decided that what you're adapting for is worth the effort.

When I first began the juggling act of school, work and dance, time management was only one of the tricky factors life threw at me. Other obstacles started to present themselves, too. For example, the times when I was available for dance classes didn't always align with the classes that were intended for my age group, meaning I sometimes had to take dance classes with students who were significantly younger than me. I was often laughed at by many people my age for taking classes with kids. There was also an instance when my favourite Saturday class got switched to a different day to make way for regional competition rehearsals. I was absolutely gutted because it was an age-appropriate class for me that didn't overlap with any of my scheduling issues, due it being on the weekend.

The easiest decision would have been to walk away and lose this dancing time, but that wasn't what I chose to do. Instead I joined the regional competition rehearsals, despite the fact that I wasn't going to be competing. During what was now rehearsal time in that Saturday slot, the dancers were practising an intense routine for the competition where each of them had to handle a door (a real, wooden door), which acted as their duet partner. They would dance on it, open and close it, lean on it, and whatever else the choreography demanded. Not being part of the competition, I wasn't given a door. Now, looking back on this time, I realise I readily applied WOOP subconsciously and adjusted it to what the current situation required. I visualised how sad I would be *if* I wasn't dancing and how much of a step back in my training it would be if I didn't carry on. So, *then* I chose to stay for the rehearsal slot, ignored what others might have thought of me, and learned the entire routine with my own invisible door. I was off to the side, dancing by myself with a door that didn't exist, for a number I wasn't in, for a competition I couldn't compete in. From an outsider's perspective, I looked nuts. To this day, my dance teacher and I reminisce about this and celebrate how much determination and resilience I had. Because, you see, that invisible door gave me very visible results later in life.

I didn't know then where or how this dedication to dance would manifest itself for me. But I believed that if I kept going and worked hard, slowly (and sometimes it would feel *very* slow) something would one day happen. In all honesty, it would be a lie to say there weren't moments when I thought to myself, 'What's the point?', but when feeling uninspired, unmotivated and overwhelmed starts to become the norm, the desire for a shift happens. In hindsight, I'm so thankful to those uncomfortable and uneasy times that led me towards a moment of stillness when I needed it. In light of the unhappiness they created, I sought out my inner voice's truth, I listened more acutely, I breathed and continued breathing until I heard what needed to be heard.

We all have the magic within us to achieve the goals we set for ourselves, but like all the best things in life, it comes with a bit of work. At the end of the day, dreams are just dreams until you start working at them; they can only ever serve you as well as you serve them. And for those who don't really know what their dream is just yet, know that this uncertainty is more than okay. It's never too late to discover a dream. By listening to that voice within and applying the WOOP technique along the way, you are guaranteed to start living a more fulfilled life, while you allow your dreams the chance to unfold.

TAKE A MOMENT

Meet yourself where you're at in this very moment. Choose to honour your present self by investing in your future self. What changes would you like to make? Again, take a breath and listen. What is your inner voice telling you or guiding you towards? Think about your own WOOP steps (see page 144). Is there a first step you can take towards your wish right now? Can you imagine an *if* and *then* scenario to help you sense what that change or goal might look and feel like for you? Write it down and slowly start to apply WOOP today. Choose to make visible the 'invisible door' in your life – even if, at first, you're the only one who seems to see it.

'Ordinary things consistently done lead to extraordinary results.'

KEITH CUNNINGHAM

FIVE, SIX, SEVEN, EIGHT!

Before every dance routine begins, without fail, you will always hear the choreographer shout, 'Five, six, seven, eight!' This serves as a reminder of the rhythm and timing of the dance, but also acts as a countdown for when the dance is meant to begin. When first learning a dance routine, much like anything else in life, it can be a little rocky. You forget steps, you go off-beat and, well, you simply make mistakes – lots of them. But, eventually, with enough rehearsal, the routine begins to feel like second nature, something that, in time, you can do with little or no thought, and that's when the enjoyment aspect of the performance comes in. One of my favourite things about my time on *Strictly Come Dancing* was experiencing the shift from where my celebrity dance partner began each week to the performance everyone then saw on show day. Seeing their faces light up as a move or sequence that once seemed impossible actually came to feel enjoyable was wonderful. You see, a dance routine remains the same every time you do it; it's choreographed to the lyrics or music and will never stray from that no matter how many times you do it. This allows the person learning it to feel a semblance of structure. And this does not just apply to dance routines; the same is true of routines in general.

Much of what happens in life is beyond our personal control, which is why having a structured routine that we know we can actively manage feels so good. I know it doesn't necessarily sound sexy to say, 'I love having a routine,' but the same feeling of personal satisfaction I get from nailing a dance routine I can also receive from the seemingly small routines I implement in my daily life. In our minds, most of us have come to associate the word 'routine' with tasks and activities that may often bring us stress or we may find boring. However, routines can be an incredibly powerful tool to buoy our mental and physical health.

While routines may feel mundane and predictable, they allow us slowly and consistently to work towards something we want to achieve or change in our lives. Which is why finding your rhythm in life can bring you the same joys as finding your rhythm in a dance. You feel not only in control, but capable.

THE JOYS OF ROUTINE

Every morning, the very first thing I try to do as soon as I wake up is take a shower. For me personally, nothing wakes me up and gets me going for the day better than a nice warm shower. As much as I wish it weren't true, I am not a morning person. However, my job often very much is – both as a presenter, and now as a mother. So, for me, an early-morning shower is just as appreciated as it is needed. After my morning shower, I go on to use my favourite skincare products and then finish my routine by making the bed. Upon that last pillow being placed, I am ready to start my day. The reason I said 'try to do' above is that some days, because of Lyra, the order of the routine changes. When Lyra is up before me, I make sure to feed her, change her nappy and play with her for a while before passing her to her daddy. BUT, as soon as that is completed, I go on to take my shower, apply my skincare and make the bed. A key thing to note here is that routine can be incorporated in an adaptable way, so that it fits your day and schedule. While the exact time stamp may not be the same for my routine every day, the feeling I get upon completing it is. Once my morning routine is done, I then feel I am ready to take on the day with a bit more zest.

The evenings also consist of their own routine. I always aim to have no screen time at least thirty to forty-five minutes before bed, meaning no late-night Instagram scrolling or YouTube videos.

Most nights, I light a candle, make my way around the house and dim all the lights. After that, I give Lyra her last feed and a little baby massage or some sort of soft play to get her ready for bedtime. Once she's asleep, I have another shower, pop on my night-time skin products and eventually unmake the bed. Then I read a little to help my mind unwind and get ready to sleep. While my night-time routine is a bit harder to follow consistently, I have found that the more often I am able to incorporate it, the better I feel for it. Routines give us a sense of control and familiarity; as humans, we naturally feel comforted by things that we know and recognise. And the routines we apply in our lives eventually go on to become habits.

By nature, our minds and bodies have an internal clock telling us when it's time to wake up and when it's time to go to sleep; a daily cycle that alternates between awake state and rest state. Similarly, we have the standardised times of day that we eat, such as breakfast, lunch and dinner – a framework we created to ensure that we could regularly refuel our bodies and have the energy we need for the day. It's through the creation and repetition of such routines that habits are formed, until eventually we perform the task without even having to think about it. It may seem contradictory, but by using routine, we ultimately create space for more freedom and flow in our daily lives. In doing things that have become second nature, rather than having to consciously choose to do them, our mental energy is freed up for other things, leading to a more present and happy life.

It sounds dull, but the key to this process is repetition. Just like life, dance will present you with struggles: not remembering a step, not being able to find the right rhythm or having difficulty learning a movement that feels foreign to your body. Yet as you practise and rehearse the routine repeatedly, eventually the choreography becomes ingrained in you, much like any habit does. Slowly but surely, you find yourself remembering steps without having to think about them, or you hear the music and naturally your body remembers the movements that are meant to accompany it. Ultimately, you begin to establish control over the dance and your body, and as a result of that intrinsic control, you begin to feel free to actually enjoy what you're doing. The power of habit, created from the consistency of repeated routine, has led you to this moment where you can be fully present in the moment of enjoying the music and the movements you have learned.

BETTER CHOICES THROUGH ROUTINE

When obstacles get in the way of life (and they frequently do), you'll find that having a sense of order and familiarity in your actions will enable you to better handle those obstacles consciously and mindfully. Routine allows this power to flourish. Going back to the dance example for a moment: if you make a mistake while dancing but are aware that you are in control because you know the steps like the back of your hand, then you can more easily adjust your moves and fix the mistake efficiently. Because routine allows us to feel in control, it also establishes a baseline sense of calm within us, and feeling calm creates a mental environment that is conducive to clearer thinking. So, in a state of calm, the mind is better equipped to weigh up different options, assess information and navigate complexities with a heightened sense of discernment, leading us to make better choices.

Routine not only allows us to feel safe when things don't go to plan, but also makes us feel more confident in our ability to take on the unexpected. When you have no routine in your life, it's easier to lean in to bad habits when things go awry. For example, establishing a routine is pivotal for individuals in addiction recovery, as it fosters a sense of peace and stability. By incorporating structure into their daily lives, they can manage urges more effectively, and also cultivate a mindset that is better suited to decision-making in those moments of uncertainty.

At present in my life, nothing is more important than Lyra's well-being. When there are sleepless nights and she's crying loudly, choosing to lean on my established routine allows me to think more clearly about any decision I have to make regarding Lyra in that moment. Through the consistency of routine, Aljaž and I are able to learn Lyra's different behaviours and better understand what she needs from us at different times. Having the ability to channel clarity in moments that feel cluttered, pressured or stressful is an invaluable tool that routine equips you with.

WHEN ROUTINE MEETS SPONTANEITY

Understand that life will not always be routine. Not at all. Some of the best moments in my personal life have been entirely spontaneous, such as the moment I found out I was pregnant with Lyra. My entire world changed. I was conscious of the fact that our day-to-day life would look very different once she came along, but Aljaž and I were thrilled and more than ready to adjust our lives and our daily routine in order to make space for her in it.

Sometimes, allowing yourself to shake things up and change your routine is just as important as having one to begin with. Having a child is a prime example of this, but these spontaneous sparks can occur in the small moments, too. Have you ever had a friend or family member convince you to go on an outing that was not in your schedule that day, and then you ended up having an incredible time?

In the rhythm of a structured routine, spontaneity becomes the delightful surprise that adds colour to everyday life. While routine provides a reassuring sense of calm during challenging times, it also magnifies the joy we can feel in those spontaneous moments. Consider the psychological principle of 'hedonic adaptation', which focuses on how, despite positive or negative events that occur, humans tend to return to our baseline level of happiness after a while.[9] Think of routine as a key player in maintaining this baseline, offering a steady stream of contentment. When we add spontaneity, it's like a burst of laughter in a quiet room – it breaks the routine in the best way possible, making life more exciting and memorable. It's within this dance between routine and spontaneity that you find the sweet spot that makes life more fulfilling.

ROUTINE AND SETTING GOALS

A huge part of making our goals a reality is achieved through routine. As previously discussed, routines help us to create habits, and habits allow us to do something without a second thought, making them an incredible asset when working towards a big life goal. When we no longer need to think about how to do something and can run almost on autopilot, we free up space in our minds to focus on other – and often more important – things.

A common thread among highly accomplished individuals is the significance of routines, particularly morning routines. Charles Duhigg, author of *The Power of Habit: Why We Do What We Do and How to Change*, underscores how our brains prioritise habits over learning new information.[10] Imagine having to relearn the intricacies of brushing your teeth daily – it would undoubtedly consume precious time. This is how habits, stored in our brains, free up mental space for more critical aspects of personal development. When it comes to our goals, regardless of their size, creating habits is key to actually achieving them; they are the small building blocks that will form the basis for the bigger edifice that we want to achieve.

Take, for instance, the simple goal of increasing your water intake. Starting with a full glass in the morning and gradually adding more throughout the day creates a routine that ensures the goal is met. Reflecting on my own experience, I remember wanting to strengthen my hair when it was looking a bit frazzled due to frequent styling for performances. So, I started taking hair-enhancing vitamins alongside my other supplements as part of my morning routine. Slowly, I began to see the strength in my hair coming back. By adding those vitamins to my morning routine, I ensured that I took them daily and therefore got the desired results.

Whether big or small, routines and habits are the roadmap for successfully achieving your goals. The only way to build a house is by adding one block at a time. The act of doing this might feel slow, ordinary or mundane, but the result is the home of your dreams. The ordinary has become extraordinary.

HOW TO CREATE ROUTINE

Creating a routine can be daunting, but it becomes more manageable when you break down the process into manageable sections. You first have to realise what you want and then create the necessary steps to action it. A notable 2009 study published in the *European Journal of Social Psychology* suggests that, on average, it takes about sixty-six days for a new behaviour to become automatic.[11] However, this is just a benchmark; the timeframe can vary widely depending on the complexity or difficulty of what you are trying to achieve. For instance, integrating a morning glass of water into our routine might be a more seamless process compared to committing to a daily routine of fifty sit-ups. Our routines demand a dedicated effort to transform them into the habits we seek. Much like rehearsing a dance routine until it flows effortlessly, the key is to persistently nurture our routines until they become second nature.

As I mentioned earlier, when I took a step back from dancing on *Strictly*, I felt a bit lost without the daily rehearsals that kept me physically active for eight to ten hours a day. That was all I'd known for so long. Having led such a consistently active lifestyle, I was worried about the impact this sudden change would have on both my body and my mental health. I also didn't want to lose my stamina and ability to perform when needed. Faced with a hectic schedule and the challenge of finding time for the gym, I decided it was time to sit down and create a routine. I knew my mornings would be ideal, seeing as in the evenings I was often either filming or at an event, and that schedule changed on a weekly basis. So, I decided to get a personal trainer and meet with her at the gym two to three times a week for some weight training in the early mornings. We scheduled our sessions depending on what I had on that week, and I stuck to it as much as possible.

Initially, getting myself to the gym was a struggle, but eventually I began to crave the energised version of me that left each session. As the weeks passed, the once-dreaded routine transformed into a genuine source of enjoyment for me. If I missed a session, it became noticeable in my mood, solidifying weight training as a valued part of my weekly rhythm. Even in the midst of intense rehearsals for the Christmas-show tour with Aljaž, I insisted on scheduling two early-morning sessions per week. Even though I was on tour dancing and being physically active every day, I had created the habit of weight training, and my body knew it. Once the habit was established, the effort it took to get up and go to the gym was a fraction of what it had been when I was first trying to create the habit.

So, to help you create your own habit, below are some tips to keep in mind when building a new routine:

First, establish your end goal. What do you want to get out of your routine? Is it a broad goal, such as feeling better overall about your day, or is there a more specific goal that you want to achieve?

Plan a routine that is realistic and doable; start small and grow it from there. There is no point in trying to add something to your day, week or month that you know would be impossible to achieve. For example, if you want to add exercise into your mornings, don't all of a sudden put pressure on yourself to go to the gym every day for an hour. Start with shorter sessions just a few times a week and build from there. It will only demotivate you if you create a routine that is not sustainable.

Be flexible. Some routines might be extremely rigid (i.e. brushing your teeth every day), but most have room for flexibility. Let's say you want to read more in the evenings. You don't need to allocate a specific time to reading every night, or read for a specific length of time either. Just making sure that you pick up a book when you get into bed, whatever time that might be, and reading for as little or as long as you like each night, is fine. Allow yourself room to be adaptive so you can better guarantee that you'll stick to it.

STICK TO IT! This is the hardest part. Remember, it takes an average of sixty-six days to create a habit. We all fall off the wagon sometimes, but making sure we get back on it will make the world of difference in creating those desired habits. Also, be sure to show yourself some grace if you do slip. The point is to keep going in spite of the setbacks. Before you know it, the routine you've created will come easily to you, and you might even find yourself missing it when you aren't able to do it.

Embracing routine in our lives is a powerful catalyst for clarity and fulfilment. It provides a familiar anchor, guiding us to make better choices, relish spontaneous moments and steadily progress towards our goals. Stability, comfort and control emerge as its gifts, allowing us to seamlessly integrate habits into our lives, seemingly without effort. As the countdown begins and I shout, 'Five, six, seven, eight!', what routine will you be choosing to establish?

TAKE A MOMENT

Equipped, now, with the information on how routine can have a huge impact on reaching your goals, is there an adjustment you can make in your own life that will help you attain what you'd like to achieve? Is there something you've been wanting to start doing, or do more of? Maybe you want to be a little more organised so you can more effectively get all your daily tasks done. Maybe you want to be outside more. Whatever it may be, start thinking of the small steps that you can action daily (at least sixty-six times, remember!), and which you can start applying to your life now. Once you begin, remember to stay flexible, but most importantly, remember to STICK WITH IT! One day soon, you will see extraordinary results.

'We can't always change what happens around us, but we can change what happens within us.'

ANDY PUDDICOMBE

STOP THE CLOCK

In the grand dance of life, time pirouettes forward, an unstoppable force with a rhythm of its own, ticking away with the constancy of a heartbeat. Time serves as our constant companion, yet in its infinite power, it remains elusive, slipping through our fingers like sand. While time can be our biggest healer, it can also be one of the hardest things to realise that time may be passing us by.

You see, time is a master of disguise. It moves in silence, an invisible maestro conducting the symphony of our lives. Have you ever found yourself en route somewhere, only to arrive with a sense of amnesia, realising that you operated entirely on autopilot, with little to no recollection of the actual drive to get there? Or, for the parents reading, have you looked at your ever-growing child and marvelled, 'Where did the time go?' It's a thought I've had, gazing at

Lyra, feeling amazed at the speed at which time operates, in awe of its fleeting magic.

However, there are a few things that can act as a time machine of sorts; things that, even if only for a moment, can transport us back to an earlier time in our lives. Consider photographs – snapshots of a single moment, which allow us to traverse time in an instant, with the ability to freeze-frame the laughter, the tears and the love – true stills of our life. The same can be said for music, strumming the chords of nostalgia. A certain song comes on and suddenly we're back to the first moment we heard it. Film offers another experience of time travel, acting as a storyteller that travels through various time periods, painting the past, predicting the future and inspiring hope for the present.

The truth of the matter, though, is that time stops for no one. It refuses to be tamed, flowing like a relentless river, a one-way stream with no U-turns. So we go with the current. We move forwards. And in its silent and invisible passage, time often eludes our notice, slipping past us like a ghost in the night, leaving us dazed, wondering where the hours went and how we could have better spent them.

Since my move to the UK in 2013, life has been a kaleidoscope of experiences – from joining *Strictly Come Dancing* to getting engaged, then married, then buying our first home and now becoming a mother. Amid so much activity, I often find myself wondering, 'Where did the time go?' It's a common reflection, and one that brings both nostalgia and joy. Consciously pausing to look back allows me to cherish every moment, so I do flip through old photographs, listen to those cherished songs or indulge in my favourite films – most of them Disney classics that transport me back to my childhood. The joy it brings me and the love that engulfs my heart when I do makes me feel so happy.

Of course, the unforeseen gift of the lockdown era was a profound opportunity to truly stop for once. In a world where our minds race at a million miles per minute, embracing stillness seems not only impossible, but also scary. Yet when we do take time to sit with that stillness, clarity emerges. Pre-COVID, my life was a whirlwind – *Strictly Come Dancing* dominated five months of the year, and tours, gigs and a cascade of events filled my days, usually from dawn till midnight. My calendar for 2019 was crammed with a plethora of commitments, leaving little room for reflection.

However, lockdown changed everything. Suddenly, we had all the time in the world. Time was still ticking away, but I now had it all to myself. Obviously, time is always ours to spend however we choose, but we rarely see it that way because the frenetic nature of life invariably takes over. Usually, we're too busy and too engulfed in doing whatever it is we 'need' to do to realise the value of time.

During lockdown, upon recognising that time is indeed ours, I set out on a personal journey of introspection.

Suddenly, time became a canvas for inner exploration, which eventually led me to the transformative wonders of meditation. This became the one thing I felt I could control during a time when there was little many of us *could* control. Now, for many people, the mere mention of the word 'meditation' can be a deterrent. It often conjures images of carefree individuals with an abundance of free time and overly flexible schedules. Most would say yes to peace, love and happiness if they felt they had the time. Well, ironically, it is precisely those individuals navigating tight schedules, a myriad of worries and colossal responsibilities for whom meditation proves to be most useful.

MEDITATION IS FOR ALL, FOR EVERYTHING

When I found myself peeling inwards during lockdown, I started taking my online well-being course offered at Yale University, for I now had the luxury of time and was curious to learn more about it. Amid my well-being studies, I began to dive deeper into the world of meditation, and it slowly began to transform my outlook in even the simplest moments. Whether I was taking a walk outside, sitting and focusing on my breath or immersing myself in music, meditation granted me a new lens through which to perceive the world. After all, true meditation, at its core, allows the world to momentarily stand still, offering complete immersion in the present moment. It's important to note that meditation is not a one-size-fits-all practice; it can be applied to all kinds of experiences. Running, for instance, became my unexpected avenue of stillness. Prior to embracing meditation, the treadmill had allowed me a moment to myself, when I had to focus solely on the rhythm of my breath, but when I added meditation into the mix, it became a more profound experience.

Admittedly, my journey into meditation wasn't a seamless one. Like many, I grappled with the relentless chatter of my mind, struggling to find respite from the constant noise of everyday existence, which was especially loud for all of us during this chaotic time. Yet, with patience and persistence, I began to unravel the labyrinth of my thoughts, embracing the ebb and flow of consciousness with each passing breath. Gradually, I learned to observe my thoughts as they floated by, starting by focusing on my breath during activities like running, stretching or lying on my bed. Meditation was by no means a quick fix; it took time before its profound impact on my mental health unfolded, especially at a time when our universal clock was ticking, nothing seemed to be changing and there were so many unanswered questions.

MEDITATION FOR THE MIND

In our bustling world, where stress, anxiety and the blues are frequent visitors, meditation stands as a truly worthwhile companion. In the whirlwind of *Strictly Come Dancing* in 2017, I found myself juggling a summer tour, wedding planning and then *Strictly* rehearsals straight after the wedding celebrations. I was paired with Aston Merrygold that year, from the boyband JLS, and the pressure to deliver each week was immense. Aston was amazing, and we are still great friends, but I couldn't help nervously feeling that I wasn't going to be good enough. My mind went into overload, overthinking every decision, second guessing every step we took on that floor. Regardless of the level of dance experience your celebrity partner had, the expectation to deliver a great routine every week can be tough. So, naturally, our early elimination hit me hard, and I grappled with the weight of responsibility. It took a long time before I came to terms with the fact that I had actually done a great job, but that much of the show was out of my control. Despite the setbacks, we went on to win the Christmas Special later that year, reminding me that sometimes the journey takes unexpected turns.

Fast-forward to 2020, when I got partnered with young popstar HRVY. My previous worries remained, but that year we had the unique set of challenges posed by COVID to contend with as well. Aljaž and I had our tour cancelled, and I had not danced in many months before going into the series, so I was nervous that I was not in my best 'dance shape' and that perhaps my creative juices wouldn't flow as easily due to having been out of the game for so long. Human as I am, insecurities arose, and I had the added pressure that HRVY and I were the bookies' favourites to win.

This time, however, I had a secret weapon up my sleeve: meditation. Daily doses of meditation became my lifeline. Whether it was the crack of dawn or the still of night, I found solace in my breath. Suddenly, the chaos felt a little less chaotic and the pressure a little less crushing. I learned to embrace the journey, to revel in the moment, no matter the outcome. And lo and behold, HRVY and I danced our hearts out, all the way to the *Strictly* final! In all honesty, meditation transformed me, body and soul. It rewired my patience, my understanding, my very essence. And as a new mum, that sense of calm is more precious to me and more appreciated than ever. It allows me to be a better mother for Lyra.

These were some of the tangible ways in which meditation helped me personally when it came to performing on the dance floor, but it can also pave the way for enhanced concentration. In the calm embrace of a focused mind, you'll find an increased ability to navigate tasks with precision and make decisions with clarity. While the morning is often touted as the ideal time for meditation, its gifts are accessible at any point during the day. If you're caught in the intricate web of work projects or feeling as if you're drowning in daily stressors, set aside just a few minutes to reconnect with your breath and engage in a mini meditation. Feel the soothing balm it offers your mind, allowing you to return to your tasks with a new-found clarity and perspective.

It's important to add, too, that when you are in a clearer state of mind, you are more receptive to and accepting of those around you. With a busy and cluttered mind, it's difficult to make space for others. Allowing that space can create deeper connections with those close to you. You are more open to listening, as well as sharing. This can help not just in your personal relationships, but in how you handle relationships at work, or even in dealing with strangers. Ultimately, there are many benefits connected with meditation; it has been shown to ease both the mind and the body. It's why we are seeing it being incorporated more and more into our work lives, our medical care and even our childcare, with some children's nurseries teaching little ones how to focus on their breathing and listen within to help them become more present and better manage stress, anxiety and other big emotions.

Common Benefits of Meditation

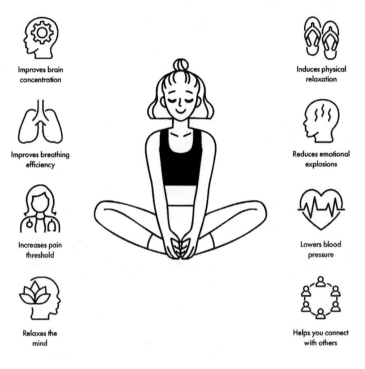

Improves brain concentration

Improves breathing efficiency

Increases pain threshold

Relaxes the mind

Induces physical relaxation

Reduces emotional explosions

Lowers blood pressure

Helps you connect with others

Now, let's address the elephant in the room. In our fast-paced, whirlwind existence, finding a pocket of silence for any substantial amount of time seems nearly impossible. Meditation does not stop the clock; time does not stand still when you focus on your breath or a mantra. Life pulls us in every direction, leaving us with fragmented moments to call our own. So, let's approach it with a healthy dose of realism. Instead of setting the bar impossibly high, why not dip your toes in the tranquil waters with a modest start? In other words, instead of putting pressure on yourself to become the next Deepak Chopra (one of my favourite figures in alternative medicine), why not start by taking just one minute for yourself every day?

TAKE A MOMENT

Try this simple meditation practice, which involves taking one minute in the morning, and one minute in the evening – just you, your breath and a moment of peace. No fancy mantras, no yoga poses required. Just a quiet moment for yourself, and a gentle nudge towards the serenity that lies within.

Place yourself in a comfortable position. It could be sitting down on a chair or on the floor, or lying face-up on your bed.

Put one hand across the middle of your chest over your heart, and the other on your stomach.

Take three seconds to breathe in, hold it for two seconds, then release the breath for four seconds. As you breathe in, fill your stomach with your breath. Feel your stomach expanding, while your shoulders and your chest remain still.

With each breath, feel your stomach expand, and try to connect to your heart. Become aware of your breathing, focusing on your counts as you inhale, hold and exhale.

Breathe out through your mouth and allow yourself to sit more fully in your body through each exhale.

Repeat these steps daily, once in the morning and once at night, for just one minute. That alone will make a difference. Once you feel comfortable, you can then start to add more minutes to your practice as you go. Before you know it, you may find yourself doing thirty minutes or an hour, purposefully making time for it in your busy schedule. And if you feel you want to try a little more, and perhaps have a guide talk you through your meditation as you get more comfortable with it, try the Headspace meditation app – one of my favourites. It's great for beginners who just want to get started and find a little more of their own inner peace.

THE PHYSICAL BENEFITS OF MEDITATION

The wonders of meditation can extend beyond a serene mind; regular practice can also boost your physical well-being. It's a known fact that high levels of stress and anxiety can result in high blood pressure, and this is one area where meditation has proved to be an effective ally, gently guiding those affected to a more stable state of health. Similarly, during a woman's pregnancy journey, maintaining calmness and focused breathing can have a major impact on anxiety levels. The deliberate act of breathing slowly facilitates the smooth flow of oxygen in the blood, creating an internal haven for both the mother and the precious life growing within.

Another physical benefit lies in meditation's ability to enhance our sleep quality, which is an indispensable pillar of our overall health. In a society where the importance of sleep is increasingly being recognised, meditation emerges as a powerful tool for promoting restful slumber. As the mind releases itself from the weight of incessant thoughts and worries, sleep becomes more attainable and rejuvenating. But here's the catch: modern technology isn't making this any easier for us. Our smartphones have become our preferred sidekicks in daily life. We spend hours upon hours every day scrolling and refreshing for new content to keep our minds busy. Not only is this constant stream of media a major roadblock for achieving mental calm, it also disrupts our body's natural sleep–wake cycle. The blue-light emissions that come from electronic devices trick our brains into thinking it's daytime even when its dark, making it much more difficult for us to fall asleep or stay asleep. But there is something we can do to combat this …

TAKE A MOMENT

I challenge you to try something different tomorrow. First thing in the morning, before you dive into the relentless whirlwind of notifications, emails and the digital hustle, allow yourself a moment to pause. Instead of reaching for your phone right away, try to resist the urge and instead engage in any other morning activity: showering, brewing a coffee, stretching or simply looking out of your window. The point is to try anything that doesn't involve the immediate stimulus of social media and online news. And here's a delightful twist: you can even try adding some background noise, perhaps as you make the bed. Play some of your favourite tunes and get those happy hormones going. Allow yourself to be fully present in those first few minutes of your day. Embrace the simplicity of this practice – it's so doable. It's not a full-blown twenty-five-minute meditation, but it helps to stop the speed of life from being the very first thing to enter your thoughts in the morning. Extend this conscious choice into your evenings. Consider designating a cut-off time for phone usage and take this time as a deliberate pause to focus on yourself. Notice the shift in your mood and how this ripple effect resonates throughout the days that follow.

TAKE A DAY

In the whirlwind of life, it's crucial to hit pause. We're all learning how to navigate the chaos, and finding those moments to check in, recalibrate and then dive back in with a clear mind is essential. Most of us have our coveted two-day weekends, and paid time off at work – these are our societal signal to stop, reset and gear up for the hustle to begin once more. But it can be all too easy to ignore these prompts.

For a long time, being busy was all I knew. To me, time well spent meant time that was booked up and busy. Back during lockdown, I recall filling my days in any way I possibly could. Each day blurred into the next as I juggled workouts, dinners, daily Instagram Lives and the perpetual quest for the latest COVID updates. It was like being on a hamster wheel, a ceaseless loop in time that left me strangely fatigued, the void within me growing more noticeable. The realisation hit hard – I needed to hit pause.

Enter my 'stop the clock' day. I made it a mission to fully switch off one day a week. I'm talking about a full-blown phone detox – no emails, no alarms, no agendas, no social media, no endless scrolling. Just me, spending a day when time feels like it's mine again. This day is dedicated to cuddles with my two constants – Lyra and Aljaž – a luxurious meditation session (if Lyra allows), immersing myself in nature, catching up with loved ones, revisiting old photos, and indulging in my favourite films and music. It's my day, and when I resurface, I'm armed with the feeling that I can conquer the world.

For me, this day of serenity usually unfolds on a Sunday, which beautifully sets the stage for a productive Monday. Having gifted myself the luxury of time on Sunday, Mondays become filled with energy and possibility. Admittedly, when I'm on tour, Sundays often entail performances, but the principle remains steadfast – designate a day for yourself, regardless of the calendar's constraints. Scrutinise your schedule and find your day. Embrace it fully, unburdened by guilt, recognising that this time is an investment in becoming the best version of yourself when you return to the daily grind. And the magic ingredient? Meditation. Initially, a mere five minutes morphed into a daily ritual for me, before gradually extending to ten, fifteen, thirty minutes, and sometimes a blissful hour. The results were nothing short of transformative. Anxiety dwindled, replaced by an insatiable hunger for well-being, exercise and creativity. Optimism emerged, illuminating the darkness that had settled from spending so much time indoors and isolated. This intentional 'stop the clock' day injected vitality into my week, setting the tone for a new-found lease of life. The momentum continued as I weaved meditation into my daily fabric; it was evident in my resilience during those seemingly endless weeks of lockdown. By mastering the art of doing nothing on Sundays and embracing daily meditation, I discovered the secret to unlocking boundless hope and positivity in the face of life's challenges.

Life has thankfully since taken a turn back to normality for all of us, so my approach to meditation and downtime has evolved from the lockdown days, yet the essence of my practice remains unchanged. In the midst of morning and evening rushes, I steal just one minute to pause and tune in to my breath. And these days, of course, my 'day off' primarily revolves around caring for Lyra – a challenging but uplifting task that fills my heart with unparalleled joy. Nevertheless, I carve out a precious fifteen minutes for myself, steering clear of the social-media and work vortex. Whether it's diving into a book, catching an episode of my latest series obsession or indulging in a bit of stretching, these stolen moments are my sanctuary. The key isn't about diving head-first into an hour-long meditation session. It's about discovering what fits neatly into your routine and gradually building on it.

My journey showcases the transformative power of allowing yourself to pause, embracing the world within, fostering mental clarity and cultivating a serene heart. These practices, carried over from the days when time was abundant into the current hustle when twenty-four hours still feel insufficient, have become the cornerstone of my own well-being. While I remain flexible regarding the frequency and length of my practice, one non-negotiable is dedicating an entire day each week to a complete break from routine and work. A day to rest the mind, rejuvenate the body and nourish the soul. It's a vital disconnection that allows me to face the challenges of the upcoming week feeling revitalised. After all, time waits for no one, but we can certainly create moments when it feels like it does.

TAKE A MOMENT

The invitation stands: take a moment to 'stop the clock' for yourself. Begin with small acts of presence – observe the trees, gaze at the sky, inhale the outdoor air deeply or fully disconnect from technology for a day. Initiate those one-minute breathing exercises (see page 178) and let the momentum build from there. Whatever method you choose, embrace the art of finding stillness in the perpetual dance of time.

PILLAR IV
DISCOVERY

INTRODUCTION

The exploration of the self that we have embarked on thus far has one definitive aspect that matters above all else: discovery. Peeling back the layers of our being to examine the intricacies of our strengths, weaknesses, darkness and light is a revelatory experience, a grand adventure into the depths of our souls, where every development uncovers a new facet of our character. In this expansive process, we find ourselves immersed in a world teeming with potential and wonder. With each step forward, we unearth hidden treasures – each one more precious than the last – delving deeper into the core of our being with insight and understanding. Yet, even as we uncover the layers that define us, there remain vast plains of undiscovered terrain waiting to be explored. Much like soaring into the sky and beyond, this journey knows no bounds. It is a voyage without a final destination, a perpetual exploration that unfolds with each passing moment.

With this also comes the beauty of discovering the bigger world around us. Whether it's a new passion, a deep connection with another person or a profound understanding of our own inner workings, every discovery we make adds richness and depth to our lives. The true magic of discovery lies in its unpredictability – the anticipation of what lies around the next corner, the excitement of uncovering secret gems that we never knew existed. It's in these moments of surprise and revelation that we truly appreciate the wonder of exploration and the boundless possibilities that lie ahead. That's the most exciting part of finding out more about yourself: the unknown.

It is through this process that we reap the rewards of the work we did in the previous pillars. After all, long-lasting joy and fulfilment is not found in the simple or obvious. We cannot find life satisfaction via a quick fix. It's through deep exploration that we can discover the true wonders of both ourselves and the world we live in, and only this can ultimately provide us with lasting happiness. I once heard life likened to an epic film – a story with a beginning, middle and end. Yet the magic lies not in fast-forwarding to the conclusion, but in savouring each moment of the unfolding narrative. Just as the joy of our favourite film lingers with us, so too does the joy we uncover through the exploration of the self. As we embark on this inward journey, we uncover dormant parts of ourselves yearning to be unleashed

– reservoirs of untapped potential ready to be harnessed, holding within them the seeds of our most authentic selves, just waiting to germinate and unfurl. It is through the act of self-discovery that we unlock the gates to these inner chambers, tapping into a wellspring of creativity, passion and purpose that enriches every aspect of our lives. And as we traverse the landscapes of our inner world, we find that the truest treasures are not found in material wealth or external accolades, but in the profound sense of peace, joy and fulfilment that comes from embracing our true selves.

'One genuine
connection can make
you feel at home in an
unfamiliar place.'

CHARLOTTE FREEMAN

WHO YA GONNA CALL?

Right before Aljaž and I had Lyra, there was a lot going on for me, both internally and externally. We had the nerves of becoming parents to deal with, my career was slowly shifting from dancing to hosting, which was very tricky to navigate, and we'd moved out of London, which was where I had felt the most at home for the previous ten years. It was a lot of changes all happening at once, and we were doing it just the two of us. And all the while, I was an entire ocean away from those I love the most in this world – and right after a worldwide pandemic. (I had to inhale and exhale for a second just writing that.)

Feeling overwhelmed had become the new norm because of the shadow that COVID had cast over all our lives. But fast-forward to our move to the countryside: a picturesque scene framed in the window of rolling hills – nature's masterpiece. Sounds dreamy, right? Well, not so much when you're sitting amid a sea of boxes, a post-move mountain range of cardboard scattered across every room. Kitchen, bedroom, guest room, even the pantry – all buried by cardboard chaos. Now, for someone who thrives on tidiness, this was a bit disheartening for me. There was stuff everywhere and my mind felt equally cluttered. I couldn't summon the energy or desire to tackle the mess, leaving me feeling drained and occasionally even a bit lonely. My spirit animal during that time was the feeling of 'meh'. Aljaž was a dream husband and partner throughout this emotional roller-coaster ride I was on; I could not have asked for better. He was the Fred Astaire to my Ginger Rogers, twirling with me through it all with unwavering support. But I wasn't expecting him to control or resolve my feelings – that wouldn't have been fair to him. This was an internal battle; it wasn't his problem to solve. 'So then, how?' I thought. 'How do I fight it?'

FEELING 'MEH'

Those days when we just feel a little 'meh' have unfortunately became more common for all of us in the years after the pandemic. Coming out of COVID, straight into life going at full speed, only to be faced with a huge cost-of-living crisis, has been daunting for everyone. So if you've found yourself feeling down regardless of the good that surrounds you, you are certainly not alone. We went from an anxious space where there was so much uncertainty, not knowing if 'normal' life was ever coming back again, to suddenly diving right back into the hustle and bustle of daily life. It's just possible that we were not prepared to jump right back on the fast train after the unprecedented years we had just experienced, but very few of us stopped to give it much thought.

On more than one occasion I certainly woke up feeling 'meh' during that time. I was unmotivated, I was sad, and Aljaž was often away for work, so I was home alone a lot – home alone in a new place, surrounded by boxes, clutter and the thought that there was no end in sight to all the things I needed to do. It was Lyra's nursery that sparked the most complex thoughts in me. I had this beautiful little miracle growing inside me, who was going to fill the house with so much life. I could not wait to meet her, and yet … looking at an empty nursery was daunting. I had no idea where to begin with it, nor even where to begin as a mother. My thoughts started to spiral and I found myself feeling so unexcited about everything: the house, motherhood, work. But I had so much to be grateful and happy for! I felt like an oxymoron. 'How can I be feeling numb when I'm healthy, I have a baby coming, I have a beautiful new home and so many wonderful things happening in my life? The boxes and clutter will be sorted soon enough. It's no big deal,' I thought to myself. But no matter how much logic I used to make sense of how I felt, the 'meh' feeling kept coming at me.

Can you relate to the word 'meh'? It's the best way for me personally to describe a negative feeling that showcases itself sometimes for no apparent reason. Have you ever woken up one morning, gone through your usual morning routine and, regardless of the day starting exactly the same as any other, felt a bit low? You try to brush it off, but nothing seems to work – not even those funny animal memes that can make us all smile. This feeling of 'meh' that happens within us does actually have a name – it's called 'languishing'.

The term 'languishing' was coined by American sociologist and psychologist Corey Keyes, and is defined as a sense of stagnation and emptiness.[12] In the mental-health spectrum, we tend to go from flourishing to despair; flourishing being an optimal level of fulfilment, and despair being at the other end as a state of ill-being, or lack of well-being. Languishing is the middle area that exists between the two. In his research, Keyes discovered that more people are in a state of languishing than depression.[13] It's the ignored middle child of mental health, and a very real thing that happens to so many of us. It simply cannot be ignored; it must be acknowledged so that we can better combat it. There is still much to be discovered about languishing, but understanding that this state does exist is the first step towards understanding it. People who are in a state of languishing are three times more likely to suffer depression, so becoming aware of it and finding ways to deal with it is instrumental to improving our well-being.

DEALING WITH 'MEH'

Now that we know what it is, how do we break free from the clutches of 'meh'? Emotions, thoughts and feelings are elusive, resistant to our attempts at control. We experience what we experience, and there is no easy way to brush off the emotional consequences and move on. Attempting to mask these emotions might seem like a skilful act, but let's not misconstrue adept concealment as a positive trait. This inclination to bury thoughts and feelings only paves the way for their resurgence later, often in a stronger and more destructive form, potentially leading to a dependence on unhealthy coping mechanisms such as alcohol, drugs, people-pleasing or detachment. So, what's the remedy? How do we shift closer to the flourishing side of our mental-health spectrum rather than descending into despair?

The very first step is acknowledgement. Recognising this 'meh' state – understanding that you are in this space to begin with and allowing yourself to sit with it – is key to unlocking it. The real transformation, however, begins with an action that seems obvious and straightforward but is often overlooked: opening up to someone. While responding to sadness or loneliness by talking to someone may sound logical, it's often one of the most challenging tasks. The reluctance to seek help stems from the fear of burdening others, creating a barrier to reaching out. Yet, when it comes to feeling 'meh', the answer becomes evident: we need to talk to one another and check in on each other. Although communicating about our emotions can be intimidating, understanding the significance of human connection during tough times is crucial. It not only lessens the fear of discussing our feelings when we need to, but also puts us in a better position to support others who might be seeking a compassionate shoulder to lean on.

Communication serves as the primary tool for addressing various mental-health challenges, whether navigating the middle ground of languishing, or grappling with the more formidable force of depression. As social beings, our survival has historically relied on a sense of belonging and interconnectedness. Sharing our thoughts and emotions, fostering open conversations and checking in on one another form the foundation of our collective well-being. It's through these connections that we find solace, understanding and the strength to navigate the intricate landscape of our mental health.

MASLOW'S HIERARCHY OF NEEDS

To understand all this a little better, let's delve into the insightful world of Abraham Maslow, a trailblazer in the realm of humanistic psychology. Maslow wasn't just your average psychologist; he was a curious mind, eager to unravel the secrets of positive mental health. His quest was unique – rather than merely dealing with the aftermath of mental-health struggles, such as depression or anxiety, he aimed to uncover preventative measures to stop them happening in the first place. In essence, he wanted to equip us with the tools to sidestep those challenging states of mind altogether. Back in 1943, Maslow crafted a remarkable five-tier model of human needs, laid out in the shape of a pyramid.[14] The bottom three layers cover our deficiency needs (D-needs) – considered the essentials – while the top two layers cover our growth or being needs (B-needs). Let's break it down, starting from the foundation.

In Layer 1, at the pyramid's base, we find the physiological needs – think food, water, sleep; the good ol' essentials of life, needed for survival. Just above that, nestling into Layer 2, are our safety needs, encompassing elements such as a secure home, employment, freedom from danger and good health. Move up a notch to Layer 3, and there's the social realm of love and belonging. This layer is all about the beauty of relationships, intimacy and connection with others. Ascending further, we reach Layer 4, dedicated to esteem. This is the space where respect, self-esteem, pride and recognition find their home. And now, brace yourself for the summit – the fifth and final layer, the pinnacle of Maslow's pyramid: self-actualisation. This is the peak, where you embark on the journey of becoming the best version of yourself, reaching your full potential. So, in the pyramid of human needs, Maslow paints a vibrant picture, showcasing not just what we require as individuals, but also the fascinating journey inwards towards self-discovery and fulfilment. It's like a roadmap guiding us towards the lofty heights of

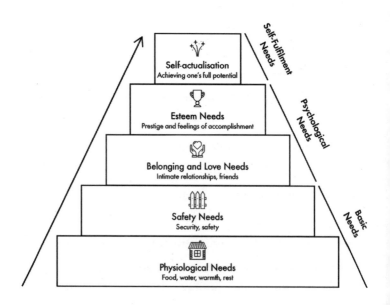

our own unique pyramids, encouraging us to scale the peaks of our personal human experience.

Imagine Maslow's Hierarchy of Needs as the blueprint for building a house – a house of self-actualisation. Just as the stability of a house relies on its foundations, so our path towards self-fulfilment relies on our core needs being met. Maslow introduced the concept of deficiency needs as the stepping stones on our climb towards self-actualisation. These aren't just checkboxes that need to be ticked before moving on; rather, they act as essential steps in the ladder. Once one layer feels satisfied, we advance to the next, creating a continuous ascent towards self-actualisation.

What captivates me most about this pyramid is the placement of love and belonging as a deficiency need. It sits at the heart of our human essentials, surpassed only by safety. The next rung in the ladder is esteem, covering elements such as self-esteem, pride and recognition. Yet, here's where it gets intriguing. Maslow's theory emphasises the significance of acknowledging love and belonging before diving into esteem. Yet we often find ourselves veering off this path, allowing esteem to take the lead and skipping over the critical need for love and belonging. It's as if we're in a rush, eager to 'get on with it', driven by our own sense of pride, low self-esteem or the fear of burdening others.

This detour from Maslow's intended order of needs can have detrimental consequences. There's a misguided belief that suppressing our need for love and connection and staying silent about it shields us from harm. But, in reality, embracing our vulnerability and fostering self-love are human strengths. It's through open communication that we find resilience and the ability to cope with the challenges that life throws our way. It's a dance of needs, and sometimes we have to let vulnerability lead the way.

MAKE THE CALL

Let's dig into the real-life effects that ignoring our need for connection can cause. Have you ever found yourself in a state where you really needed someone to talk to, yet the thought of bothering anyone with your problems or exposing your vulnerabilities held you back? That feeling of being alone in your struggles, trying to figure out how to deal with your emotions without anyone to lean on – we've all been there. While handling our feelings internally might work momentarily, adopting this approach consistently can gradually leave us feeling more isolated and trapped in our own thoughts. Ultimately, it's just not sustainable. It's essential to understand that embracing vulnerability is a strength, not a weakness. Being okay with feeling exposed is a testament to your resilience. It's about making that call, reaching out to someone when you need to and recognising that vulnerability is not a solitary experience but a shared one.

Choosing to trust others with your vulnerability in return allows them to feel safe enough to do the same. Returning to my own experience of feeling a bit 'meh' when we first moved into our new home, when that sea of unpacked boxes and the weight of change had left me feeling almost numb, it was a struggle to admit to myself then that I needed to reach out. However, understanding Maslow's Hierarchy of Needs highlighted to me the importance of love and belonging. So, I made the calls – to Aljaž, to my parents and to my siblings. Just a few simple conversations, and the shift was palpable. Allowing myself to be vulnerable, to talk about my feelings – it was a game-changer. As soon as I got off the phone, I felt rejuvenated and excited about our new adventures. I felt ready to tackle the tasks at hand.

For me, it was Aljaž and my family, but your lifelines could be anyone – a friend, a neighbour or even a stranger with whom you've shared a coffee-shop conversation and who gives you a good vibe. And if talking more personally face-to-face is outside your comfort zone, there are numerous services that are ready to lend an ear during those moments when you feel there's no one else to talk to (see Resources, page 255). Always remember, you are never truly alone. The fear of expressing those 'meh' feelings loses its grip the moment you voice them. Take the power away from those grey moments by giving them an outlet. It might feel daunting, but the scarier option is letting those thoughts and feelings simmer underneath, unexpressed and in isolation, where they grow ever more ferocious.

Vulnerability and the need for human connection are as vital to our survival as food and water – a truth backed up by Maslow's Hierarchy of Needs. In supporting one another, we thrive, reducing the risks of depression, anxiety and loneliness. The dangerous middle ground where we can so easily languish becomes less frightening when we actively address the deficits in our mental well-being.

Likewise, when we engage in this emotional openness, a wonderful thing happens: it extends to those around us in a reciprocal exchange. So if someone opens up to you, take a moment to listen. In our busy lives, creating the space to support someone who is brave enough to share their feelings can have a profound impact – on them, and on you. Loneliness, overwhelm, anxiety, 'meh' – we all grapple with these emotions at different points. So let's try giving and encouraging sincere responses to the common question, 'How are you?' Let's normalise reaching out. Let's foster a culture of open communication to make room for conversations that matter. If it's been a while since you connected with a loved one, a simple message or a phone call could make all the difference. Imagine the impact if everyone took a moment to check in on someone else, creating a ripple effect of compassion. Making the call – whether you need someone to talk to or you're reaching out to someone else – is always the right choice.

From personal experience, I can assure you that I've never received a message or call for a simple check-in and felt annoyed by it. Instead, I felt cherished and valued. When I've made those calls myself when I've been in need, I've always emerged feeling better, never worse.

Remember that feeling 'meh' is a valid state, and it's more common than you might think. Picture your mental well-being as a seesaw, constantly teetering between flourishing and despair, with the languishing state sitting in the middle. When we find ourselves languishing, placing more weight on the flourishing side of the seesaw through a simple phone call can help tip the balance in your favour. Catch it early, make the call and watch as the weight on your mental health starts to lift. Our mental-health journey should be a shared experience, so let's embrace the beauty of human connection, support each other when times are tough and help one another thrive. Life's baggage is infinitely lighter when it's shared.

TAKE A MOMENT

Think of someone now who you cherish but have not spoken to in a while. Can you send a quick message to check in and say hello? Know in your heart that this will make the person on the other end of that message smile; it will not feel like a bother at all. Perhaps they have been waiting for someone to get in touch. It might impact their entire day in a way that you could never have imagined and encourage them to open up. Change the narrative of mental-health conversations by igniting the ripple effect of compassion.

Similarly, if there is something that you have been wanting to share, or a weight in your heart that needs lifting, do not be afraid to make the call to someone you trust. You will not be a burden. Your feelings and emotions are valid and experienced by so many. You are not alone, and do not need to feel alone. The sooner you make the call, the sooner you will take away the power from those negative feelings. Gain control of your thoughts again and allow a friend or even a stranger to be there for you, in the same way that I know you have been there for someone else. We are all in this life together; we are never truly alone.

'Memories are timeless
treasures of the heart.'

UNKNOWN

PRESENCE OVER PRESENTS

Allow me to transport you for a moment to the ever-enchanting Slovenia, a beautiful country that, to me, feels like the embodiment of the word serenity. If you haven't had the chance to experience its charm yet, it's definitely an adventure I would recommend you embark on. So, let me whisk you away to one of my fondest memories of Slovenia, when we were nestled in the picturesque glamping resort known as Chocolate Village. I vividly recall being outdoors and sitting beside Aljaž as we listened to the gentle melody of birds singing, the soothing rush of the river and even the distant noises of a family of swans. During this time, Aljaž and I were enjoying what we affectionately labelled our 'babymoon'. Admittedly, this term was new to me, but the idea of stealing some precious moments to ourselves before we welcomed our little Lyra and our lives were transformed sounded like pure bliss. After all, our journey to parenthood had been marked by a kaleidoscope of changes. We had only recently made our move from the heart of London to the countryside of Cheshire in the North of England – a shift from a snug two-bedroom flat to a spacious four-bedroom house – and all amid the whirlwind of preparations for the baby. Setting up our new life up north was going to keep us very busy, so this little trip away was just what the doctor ordered, allowing me and Aljaž to be just us two, one last time.

The joy of our retreat wasn't just about spending time together as a couple. We also shared in the laughter of family – the playful antics of our nieces Zala and Tisa, the daughters of Aljaž's sister, and the comforting presence of his parents. The air buzzed with love, and our hearts swelled with gratitude for this perfect blend of tranquillity and togetherness. As we soaked up our time there, the looming stress of preparing the house for our little one's arrival seemed to shrink. Instead of feeling like a burden, this responsibility was now cloaked in excitement. A delightful frisson of anticipation now infused our thoughts of the preparations ahead, transforming what could have been stressful into moments of unbridled joy. Our holiday, you see, was not just a pause; it was a reviving elixir, the little boost we needed before we ventured into the uncharted waters of parenthood. In this lies the beauty of holidays. They are not just fleeting escapes; they are architects of happiness – true builders of memories.

PRESENCE OVER PRESENTS

I don't think I've ever met someone who didn't enjoy going on holiday. Even I, with a job that fills my days with purpose and fulfilment, find myself drawn by the allure of vacations. Which is why, as I sat in Slovenia, I sought to seize every fleeting second, well aware that in just a few days I'd be back in the rhythm of my everyday reality. Think of the last moment you felt really present, whether on holiday or in a certain place or situation that radiated happiness; the last moment that made you feel the utmost joy. We all crave more of those moments.

Of course, holidays always feel too short, so we try to squeeze every last drop of joy from those fleeting moments. It's a universal experience that I'm sure will resonate with many of you – an acknowledgement that these brief interludes of escape elevate our spirits and leave us yearning for more. So the question is, why do we only cherish those happy snapshots in memory, rather than allowing ourselves to craft more chapters of joy? Why does the grass feel greener in other moments? This feeling doesn't have to exist solely within the confines of a holiday or travel – you're alive in the 'now', and these are your moments. Try to look around you every day at least once and notice something beautiful, then take the mental picture and commit it to memory. In relishing the extended moments of euphoria you can experience in the smaller moments of life, you allow the holiday that is your life to feel perpetually in motion.

THE HEDONIC TREADMILL

This takes us back to the term 'hedonic adaptation' (see page 160) – the idea, formed by researchers in the field of well-being psychology, that we have a set baseline level of happiness that we always return to after either a negative or positive event. Many also refer to it as the 'hedonic treadmill', where we sprint towards the next big thing, only to find ourselves stationary in the pursuit of lasting happiness, much like a merry-go-round of desires and satisfaction. For example, imagine you finally get your hands on the latest iPhone you've been after. Oh, the excitement! The novelty! Yet, as the days turn into months, that initial thrill wanes, replaced by a subtle longing for the next shiny gadget to capture your attention. This is the hedonic treadmill in action – a relentless cycle of craving and adaptation that permeates every aspect of our lives, from the material to the intangible. Take, for instance, the ebb and flow of life's fortunes. You downsize your living space due to rising rents – not an ideal situation, but you adapt and you make it work. That's the thing about us humans: we're remarkably resilient, capable of adjusting to both the peaks and valleys of existence. Yet therein lies the rub: our adaptability, while a clever survival mechanism, often morphs into a relentless quest for the next big thing.

A large house, a nice car, great shoes (I'm a shoe girl myself), the newest phone model – all these things can give you a sense of instant gratification. However, just as quickly as the thrill came, we get used to it, returning to our base-line level of contentment, often leaving us with a desire to move on to the next thing we deem to be bigger or better. Ultimately, we're forever running on this hedonic treadmill, as described by Philip Brickman and Donald Campbell in their 1971 article 'Hedonic Relativism and Planning the Good Society'.[15] They shed light on our perpetual pursuit of an elusive happiness – a pursuit that often leaves us stranded, forever chasing an unattainable pinnacle of contentment. The biggest problem with hedonic adaptation lies in its relentless presence. It's a persistent companion, etched into our cognitive processes as a survival mechanism to keep us chasing the next food source or a better cave for winter. But in a modern life, when most of us are neither hunting nor gathering, this restlessness just brings us down. So, the million-dollar question: how do we jump off this incessant treadmill of desire, so that we can stop fruitlessly chasing a shimmering mirage? How do we find contentment in a world that perpetually whispers 'more, more, more'?

EXPERIENCE VS POSSESSIONS

Scientific studies have investigated ways of curating enduring happiness in order to resist the whims of hedonic adaptation. Imagine this process as a choreographed sequence of conscious decisions that leads to an enchanting performance of lasting contentment. The first step is for us to arm ourselves with awareness. The savvy sorcerers of advertising are well acquainted with hedonic adaptation, weaving their spells to make us believe we perpetually 'need' the thing that they are selling. Yet simply acknowledging that our latest purchase might soon morph into yesterday's trend can be transformative. With this knowledge under our belts, we can slowly become practitioners of mindful spending, opting for investments that truly resonate with our values. Suddenly, the allure of constantly craving the next acquisition loses its spellbinding grip.

Another suggestion, and the most effective action we can take, is to shift our focus to the pursuit of experiences over possessions. Choosing to do this can cause a huge shift in our overall happiness levels, because little do we realise that with each memory forged, our happy hormones perform a jubilant dance, leaving permanent imprints on our hearts. The transient joy induced by material possessions pales in comparison. Take, for instance, those incredible shoes you adore. They'll bring fleeting happiness until the next pair beckons, which means that their lifespan of making you content has an expiration date. But a cherished holiday? Ah, now there's a treasure trove of everlasting joy that you can revisit and draw from again and again.

Travel back with me to the simplicity of childhood, when our pockets may have been light but our hearts brimmed with the promise of delightful adventures – in my case, at the Walt Disney World Resort in Florida. In a world clamouring to jump on the latest trends, my parents (unwittingly wise) invested in experiences rather than possessions, and so, Mickey Mouse became the harbinger of our cherished family memories. Amid parades and rides, bonds of laughter and wonder were forged, lighting up my soul with the lasting glow of joy. Unbeknown to my parents, each trip served as a gentle shield against the monotony of habitual hedonic adaptation, bestowing upon me and my siblings the gift of enduring happiness.

I felt that our 'babymoon' in Slovenia did the same. Indeed, the very fact that we know a holiday will end only adds to the allure and happiness that it brings us; that's where the magic lies. The knowledge that all good things must come to an end adds a pinch of sparkle to the experience. Think about it: we adore vacations precisely because they're over too soon. If life were one long holiday, hedonic adaptation would swoop in and swipe the joy right from under our noses.

Savouring life's special moments in this way – as champ-
ioned by my parents – is the key to collecting memories that
will withstand the passage of time. The same can be said for
reminiscing about moments with loved ones who are no
longer with us. Memories shared together through experience will give you more to keep with you in your heart than
a gift ever will. Now, as a mother, I look forward to taking
Lyra to Disney World and creating all kinds of beautiful
core memories for her to hold on to as well.

TAKE A MOMENT

Recall a specific memory that brings you joy – a snapshot from a favourite vacation, perhaps. Take yourself
back to that moment, or even pull up a few photos on
your phone. Look at those photos and relive those
memories. Pay attention to what happens within. Feel
that wave of joy?

Memories don't merely sparkle; they endure, casting
a perpetual glow. Looking back at a photograph from
a fond trip will always bring a smile to your face, no
matter how much time has passed. A beautiful memory
of a wonderful experience is completely immune to
hedonic adaptation, and therein lies its power.

SAVOURING

Now, let's dive deep into another way we can loosen the grip of hedonic adaptation – enter the notion of 'savouring', a term coined in 2007 by psychology researchers Fred Bryant and Joseph Veroff to express the use of thoughts and actions to increase the intensity, duration and appreciation of positive experiences and emotions.[16] It is the act of stepping outside an experience, to review and appreciate it. In essence, savouring is finding the joy in life's simple pleasures by being fully present within them.[17] It could be the first bite of your favourite meal, marked with an 'mmm' of delight. However, this practice extends way beyond cuisine, inviting us to immerse ourselves in the everyday and all it offers. Imagine yourself enjoying the pleasure of a morning walk in a green space. Feel the breeze on your skin, listen to the soothing sounds of the birds, breathe in the scent of the morning freshness. It's within these ordinary yet intimate moments that you can allow yourself to find joy. Savouring, you see, is not meant to be reserved for grand occasions, but instead to act as a torch, illuminating the mundane with the warm glow of happiness. Often, we try to capture these magic moments with our phones, in a frozen picture-perfect snapshot – that's a bit of savouring right there. But here's the thing: you don't need a camera lens to savour something special. Sometimes, it's about putting the phone away and immersing yourself completely in the present moment. What's so incredible about savouring is that you can do it anywhere, anytime – there's no need for you to be on holiday. Choosing to revel in the simple details of the everyday creates a little pocket full of joy, one that you have unlimited access to. Life is a series of small pleasures, so don't forget to relish them.

NEGATIVE VISUALISATION

Have you ever had someone toss the phrase 'it could be worse' your way in the midst of an unpleasant moment? Turns out, there's a hidden gem in that phrase – a little something known as 'negative visualisation', which can act as a mental reset button that is especially handy for tackling hedonic adaptation. Negative visualisation boils down to picturing the downside of a good thing – in other words, imagining life without it and then sensing the void it would leave behind. In the throes of a busy, fast-paced life, it's easy to take things for granted: your home, your car, your job, even your loved ones. We forget that if we were to lose any of these things, it would hit us hard – very hard. Negative visualisation acts as an antidote to this amnesia; it tugs at the heartstrings, reminding us of the wonderful things we already have in our lives, giving us a nudge to rekindle the appreciation we once had for them, and regifting the feelings we had when they were first acquired. This may all sound a bit intense at first, but let's put it into practice …

TAKE A MOMENT

Imagine that right at this very moment your trusty phone decides to call it quits. No more texting, no more scrolling online, nada. How does that make you feel? Perhaps there's a pang of sadness, a sense of disconnection, a tinge of anxiety? However, the thought of losing all those memories tucked away in your device hits differently, doesn't it? By giving your phone the 'what if it's gone?' treatment, you'll notice how much more you savour having and using it afterwards.

Turns out, even a simple shift in perspective can transform your relationship with the seemingly mundane, and it isn't exclusive to material possessions. It can work wonders when applied to experiences, too. Whether you're soaking up a special moment with a loved one or finding joy in your work, try envisaging a scenario in which you're not part of that experience. Suddenly, the moment gains layers of value in your heart.

THE CLOSET OR THE SUITCASE?

Material possessions have a knack for bringing us joy. Who doesn't dream of owning their ideal house, a sleek car or a pair of kicks that just ooze style? And please note, there is absolutely nothing wrong with wanting more. We all like to treat ourselves and have something to aspire to. In fact, I plead with you to dream bold and big, and to fight to obtain what you long for. However, we must tread carefully. As we've learned, the thrill that these prizes offer is fleeting, and the joy comes to an end much sooner than you think.

The fact is, living a life of joy and fulfilment doesn't rely on those dreams being realised. You have everything you need right now in this moment to feel content. My sister Lesly, who may be young in years but whose heart is over-flowing with wisdom, loves to say 'Presence over presents' – a phrase that so fittingly encapsulates the essence of all this. Presents may give us transient delight, but the richness of being truly present in life's joyful, meaningful moments gives us happiness that lingers on.

In this chapter we've learned that, although we might never entirely bid adieu to hedonic adaptation's sneaky whispers, there is an arsenal of small yet powerful tools we can use to combat its affects and forge a more fulfilling existence. So immerse yourself in the beauty of a fleeting moment, savour those heart-to-heart conversations, relish that walk in the park or the excitement of packing for that long-awaited adventure. These, my friends, are the architects of lasting happiness, overshadowing any short-term pleasure that a crowded closet or lavish home may promise.

And so, I leave you with the following question: what will you choose, the closet or the suitcase? Will you opt for the closet, where a pair of shoes may briefly ignite your joy before fading into the shadows collecting dust? Or will you reach for the suitcase – whether tangible or metaphorical – a symbol of embracing experiences over possessions? In choosing the latter, you unfurl a lifetime of memories, an everlasting wellspring of joy from which to draw, sip and savour. Choose wisely.

'When life throws you
lemons, switch it up
and grab a banana.'

JANETTE

LEMONS AND BANANAS

My favourite fruit in the world has always been bananas. I confess, I have turned this yellow treat into an essential side-kick to virtually any dish, whether it's rice and beans or – my personal favourite – the unconventional pairing of bananas with spaghetti, one I learned in my childhood and still do today. I just can't help it; bananas make me happy. As I've grown older, my quirky banana-eating habits have become a running joke among my friends, but you know what? This joke happens to taste delicious, so I embrace it. But there's more to bananas than meets the eye. Did you know that they are considered the ultimate happy fruit? This is not just a coincidence; they're packed with the amino acid tryptophan, which the body converts into the neurotransmitter chemical serotonin – a natural mood booster. So, who's laughing now?

But a banana obsession is just the tip of the iceberg when it comes to the quirky side of yours truly. Let's rewind to my childhood, where playing imaginative games with my cousins was the highlight of my existence. Teacher, spy, adventurer and, yes, even a banker (little did I know I'd end up living that one out) – as a kid, my imagination knew no bounds. We'd transform our bedrooms into elaborate mazes using every sheet available, or create an entire department store with toys and household items for a shopping extravaganza. Each game, each world, was a unique adventure. Those were the golden days. I could be anywhere and anyone, all at the drop of a hat.

Yet, as we grow older, life's responsibilities take centre stage, and the boundless imagination of childhood begins to hibernate. We craft our neat little boxes, bound by their own set of rules, and slot life into them. Maybe that's why I clung to performing – playing games on a grander stage was a way to keep the child in me alive. But life, my friends, doesn't stay put in the confines we create for it, so why do we insist on boxing ourselves in? I say, let our imaginations out to play every now and then. Who knows what incredible feats we might achieve if we let our creativity run wild? Life is an unpredictable masterpiece; let's not try to make it fit into a frame. After all, there's nothing wrong with a grown-up who still finds joy in life's whimsical possibilities.

JUST BECAUSE

Ah, the age-old advice: 'Think outside the box.' It's a phrase that gets thrown around when we're trying to solve a problem, brainstorm a creative idea or break free from the usual routine. It's liberating, isn't it? To throw away the rule book and let the unexpected results spark a new direction or a different kind of thinking. Yet, what if thinking outside the box wasn't just a problem-solving tool? What if it became a way of life, a mantra for injecting spontaneity and joy into our everyday lives? Taking a break from the daily grind, treating ourselves to a vacation or embracing moments 'just because' can be incredibly powerful. Imagine experiencing the kind joy of that a holiday brings you, not just once a year, but scattered throughout your days, weeks and months. It's about finding fulfilment in the little things, the random acts that bring a smile to your face. And here's a thought: what if these spontaneous escapades, which have no specific reason behind them, could impact your career positively as well as your mental health? What if they could contribute to your financial well-being and catapult you into exciting opportunities?

My own life has been peppered with these 'just because' moments – when I threw myself into that musical theatre programme at the tender age of twelve, for example; not for any practical reason, but simply for the sheer joy of singing, acting and dancing. Performing on the Saturday-night show *Sábado Gigante* became a delightful outcome of that choice. Through high school, I continued my explorations, joining the drama club and a television production programme. Morning announcements, filming various projects and keeping my grades nearly perfect – these were all endeavours I embraced in high school without a roadmap to show me where they might lead.

At university, where my high grades had granted me a full scholarship to study finance, I had elective courses at my disposal, so I ventured into psychology, driven by an innate curiosity about the human mind, and Spanish for Spanish speakers, just for the love of improving my language skills. Later, I took a detour into religious analysis, not because it aligned with my degree, but purely out of a personal interest in understanding diverse cultures and their belief systems. And of course, amid the finance courses and banking responsibilities, dance remained a constant in my life. Ballet, jazz, contemporary, flamenco, pointe, hip-hop, Latin – I dipped my toe into every dance style imaginable. To fund my dance classes, I struck a deal with the studio owners, teaching and choreographing in exchange for my lessons.

Over the years, my quest for knowledge has certainly led me through a diverse array of subjects. But it was this variety of interests, this willingness to embrace the 'just because' moments, that kept my creative juices flowing. It's quite the eclectic mix, isn't it? You might be wondering, 'How on earth do all these subjects tie together in one person's life?' It's a valid question. Most students opt for a specific degree path, focusing their studies on the courses pertinent to their chosen field. And rightly so – this approach has produced remarkable doctors, lawyers, scientists and more. These professions demand a dedicated trajectory of study. However, there is still room for variation within them, often leading to specialised certifications and expertise. Consider the distinction between a paediatrician and a heart surgeon, or the nuanced differences between business law and marital law. The paths are distinct, yet interconnected, allowing for exploration within each domain.

So where do my myriad interests fit into this narrative? I approached my educational journey with a different mind-set. Rather than fixating on a singular path, I followed my curiosity and passions, much like I did as a child. Psychology, for example, beckoned because it offered a refreshing departure from the rigours of ballet. It was my escape just as much as dance was, a brief respite from the demands of work and everyday life. Engaging in dance and other courses purely out of interest provided me with moments of escapism, allowing me to disconnect from the pressures of daily life and instead indulge in pursuits that brought me joy. As time unfolded, dance and television took centre stage, but the seeds of my varied interests continued to bear fruit. In the worlds of dance and television, I discovered that each facet of my eclectic education contributed in unexpected ways. From psychology to Excel spreadsheets, from community service to Spanish-language proficiency – every experience, every skill, found its place in the intricate mosaic of my life's journey.

Sure, I've always been curious and something of a busy bee, but more importantly, this diversity of experience has made me a happy busy bee. So I invite you to consider: what could similarly spontaneous, 'just because' decisions unlock for you? Could they be the keys to a more fulfilling and joyful life? Think about it; life is too short for monotony. Sometimes, the sweetest surprises come from stepping outside the box just because you can. And therein lies the beauty of exploration – it's not about the destination, but the discoveries we make along the way.

SKILL STACKING

Let's now delve into the fascinating concept of skill stacking. Imagine it as crafting your own unique blend of abilities, like mixing ingredients to create the perfect dish. Instead of channelling all your efforts into mastering just one skill, you cast your net wider, dabbling in a diverse array of competencies. Just as you might assemble a versatile toolbox so you're equipped to deal with all manner of tasks, so each skill adds its own special flavour to your repertoire. Consider the legendary Steve Jobs, the visionary mind behind Apple. He famously enrolled in a calligraphy course during his time at Reed College in the US, purely out of curiosity. Little did he know that this seemingly random choice would revolutionise the world of technology, paving the way for the multitude of fonts and styles we enjoy today. Jobs's eclectic skill stack wasn't about collecting credits or ticking boxes; it was about indulging his curiosity and sparking innovation in unexpected ways, and because he allowed himself to feed this curiosity, it became something that set him apart.

In today's fast-paced world, skill stacking is gaining traction among the luminaries of the life-coaching realm. Figures including Jay Shetty and Steven Bartlett extol its virtues, recognising its power to enhance adaptability and value in an ever-evolving job market. In a landscape where versatility is prized, the ability to wear multiple hats – writer, editor, producer – can transform a solitary contributor into a one-person powerhouse.

My journey into professional dancing at the age of twenty-three seemed worlds apart from the fields of psychology and finance. Yet, as I soon discovered, the principles I learned in those seemingly disparate fields became invaluable assets in my creative pursuits. Psychology offered me insights into human behaviour, nurturing my ability to collaborate effectively in diverse settings. Whether I was navigating the dynamic personalities of theatre casts or juggling roles behind the scenes, adaptability was key. Meanwhile, my foray into finance and spreadsheet wizardry wasn't just a bank-bound affair; it was a lifeline in the unpredictable world of artistic endeavours. Budgeting became second nature, ensuring financial stability amid fluctuating paycheques. With Excel as my trusty sidekick, I could track my expenses, save for future adventures and strike a balance between artistic passion and fiscal responsibility. So, the next time you're tempted to pigeonhole yourself into a single skill set, think again. Embrace the art of skill stacking – a symphony of diverse talents harmonising to enrich your professional journey and elevate your craft. After all, in a world brimming with possibilities, why settle for a single note when you can compose your own masterpiece?

TAKE A MOMENT

For some it may not be so simple as just getting up and trying something new. Perhaps you need some guidance to help you explore other avenues. If you feel like you're just doing one thing, and you want to start trying out other skill sets, there are steps you can take to slowly broaden your toolkit:

Start with your current skills: What are you innately good at? Do you thrive based on your people skills? Are you super-techy? Perhaps you are an incredible organiser. Think about the qualities that are obvious to you, and lean into them.

Look for complementary skills: These are things that are directly related to your current skills. If you are a good photographer, perhaps consider learning the basics of directing. Alternatively, let's say you are an amazing accountant, so maybe learn more about quality customer service. Accounting is all about numbers, but those numbers are people's lives. The better you can communicate with clients, the more you might get out of your position. The idea is to add colour slowly to what you are already good at.

Look at multi-purpose skills: These are skills that can work across the board for varied things. For example, if you have a small business, it may be worth learning more about social-media influencing. It may have nothing to do with what your business is, but it will help your business grow, and you can network and connect with like-minded individuals who may be able to broaden your opportunities.

Set goals: Once you start learning a new skill, have in mind what you want to achieve. Keeping track of your progress will ensure that you complete it. Also, seeing your progress will keep you motivated, incentivising you to keep the momentum going.

THE POSSIBILITIES

Embarking on new ventures is like setting sail on a sea of possibilities. You never quite know where the winds of curiosity will take you, but, oh, the places you might go! Take the example above and imagine you're an accountant dabbling in a customer-services course. Suddenly, you're not just crunching numbers – you're navigating the intricate waters of human interaction, blending your accounting acumen with new-found people skills. Who knew numbers could lead to such delightful conversations? My foray into the realm of well-being was a dive into uncharted waters, prompted by the tumultuous times of COVID. Driven by curiosity and a genuine interest, this exploration became a lifeline for coping with stress and anxiety. The tools I acquired during this pursuit have not only shaped my personal life, but have seamlessly integrated into my professional endeavours as well.

Take, for instance, my nerve-racking stint on *Strictly Come Dancing* in 2020 with my celebrity dance partner, HRVY. Amid the usual pressures of being a professional dancer on the show, the added challenge of pandemic-induced restrictions loomed large. Thanks to my understanding of well-being, I weathered the storm and made it to the final, emerging stronger and more resilient for it. Little did I anticipate that my eclectic skill set would prove instrumental in my career trajectory that very same year. Hosting the BBC's *Morning Live* alongside my dear friend Gethin Jones was a dream come true. As I stood before the camera, the echoes of my high-school morning announcements and television-production classes reverberated in my mind. Pinching myself at the realisation that hosting was a passion I had nurtured for years, I recognised the synchronicity at play. Landing the role on *Morning Live* was not just a coincidence; it was a culmination of skill stacking and years of honing the craft. It's a testament to the joy you can find in the journey, when unexpected twists transform skills into stepping stones that lead you towards new-found heights.

A STORY OF 'JUST BECAUSE'

In the vibrant world of *Strictly Come Dancing*, my journey took a surprise turn in 2014. Amid the cha-cha-chas and the waltzes, I ventured into the land of YouTube, creating weekly vlogs entitled 'Janette's *Strictly* Peek'. It was a light-hearted glimpse behind the scenes, a chronicle of my week on the show. Little did I know, these humble beginnings in interviewing and presenting would evolve into a significant exploration of my passion. As the years unfolded, my commitment to refining these skills intensified. The project grew with 'Talks with Janette', a series of one-on-one inter-views with celebrities, fellow pros and various show contrib-utors. Each interaction was an opportunity to learn. While it wasn't a paid venture and cost me both time and money, it was a labour of love, a step into the unknown that might, one day, pay dividends. Then came the pandemic. Lockdown – an unforeseen pause – became an opportunity to inno-vate. Instagram Live emerged as the stage for impromptu interviews, allowing me to bring fascinating individuals I'd encountered on *Strictly* into the spotlight. These candid conversations became a lifeline, both for me and the viewers trapped in their homes. The routine of connecting, learning and entertaining became a ray of sunshine for me in those challenging times.

I had no idea my efforts were being watched, but soon the producers of *Morning Live* beckoned, offering an unexpected yet exhilarating hosting role on the show. The high-school student who had once nervously delivered morning announcements could scarcely believe the twist her story had taken.

Of course, hosting *Morning Live* turned out to be a gateway to more incredible opportunities. The producers of *It Takes Two* were captivated by my hosting on *Morning Live*, leading to yet another dream phone call. Hosting these shows became more than just a career move; it was a culmination of the fun and curiosity that had fuelled my skill stacking over the years. Today, as I stand at the helm of *It Takes Two* and as a team player on *Morning Live*, the pieces of this intricate puzzle fit seamlessly together. *Morning Live*, with its focus on overall well-being, aligns with my profound interests, while *It Takes Two* keeps me in sync with my dance roots and passions. What began as a whimsical pursuit has now shaped the next chapter of my life, each skill stacking upon the other to form a portfolio that is uniquely mine.

BRINGING BACK CHILDHOOD JOY

Beyond the career-enhancing advantages of honing a diverse set of skills, there lies the profound benefit of elevating your overall happiness quotient. Serotonin, endorphins, oxytocin – the very hormones that fuel our sense of joy – can surge when we engage in activities simply because they bring us delight. While jetting off to a glamorous holiday destination undoubtedly nourishes the soul, we can cultivate happiness through simpler, more accessible means, enriching our lives in everyday moments.

Consider the activities that ignite your spirit. Is it the strokes of a paintbrush, the solace of a long walk or the magic of a captivating film? Perhaps it's the cathartic release of writing or the fulfilment of lending a helping hand to a charitable cause. In a world steeped in structured plans and predetermined outcomes, it's crucial to indulge in pursuits purely for the joy they bring – unfettered by logic or expectation. Embrace the childlike wonder that once fuelled your excitement for life's adventures. In the wake of the pandemic, many individuals found themselves reassessing their priorities, seeking fulfilment beyond the confines of their daily routines. This awakening spurred a surge in entrepreneurial ventures and career changes, charged by a desire to align one's life with passion and purpose. Yet, the pursuit of happiness need not entail a complete upheaval of our professional lives. By reconnecting with the sources of joy that resonate with us, we can infuse our daily existence with a profound sense of contentment.

In embracing these life-enhancing activities, we often find ourselves immersed in a state of 'flow' – a concept that holds a special place in my heart. Flow, characterised by unwavering focus on a single task, transports us to a head-space of pure concentration – a state of being 'in the zone'. As children, our imaginations effortlessly took us into this flow state, where the boundaries of reality blurred in the embrace of creativity and wonder. As adults, the pursuit of this elusive state wanes amid the demands of adulthood. However, by engaging in activities that kindle our curiosity and spark joy, we can unlock the gateway to flow.

Rediscovering the joys of childhood isn't just a nostalgic trip back in time; it's a powerful elixir for our well-being. Embracing the whimsy of 'just because' activities not only elevates our happiness, but also nurtures our motivation, fosters creativity and enhances emotional regulation, making us better able to express ourselves, react to things and find clarity. And remember, just as I found in my own life, rummaging in the cupboards of creativity and curiosity and seeking out the activities that bring you flow can do more than just cultivate a happier, more fulfilled version of yourself. The rich mix of experiences, colours and skills you'll acquire can open doors to unforeseen opportunities, ones that may be beyond your wildest dreams.

TAKE A MOMENT

Think of the activities that make your heart sing. What are they? When was the last time you did them? Can you carve out space for them in your life? Ask yourself these questions, and then allow yourself the time and space to hopefully fall into your own flow state and experience the child-like joy of doing something 'just because'. In our busy existence, it's important to prioritise these moments, for they hold the key to a life well-lived.

DECORATE YOUR BOX

Remember how we talked earlier in this chapter about the importance of thinking outside the box (see page 225)? The boxes we create in our lives are traditionally square, safe and functional – a necessity for survival. But imagine your box as a canvas painted with multiple hues, an eclectic palette that evolves throughout your life's journey. While the shape and functionality of your box remain intact, it's the joyous infusion of colours and the unique elements you add to it that will make you smile whenever you reflect upon it. Revel in the vibrancy of your personal box, cherishing the things you add to it that spark joy, just because they do.

As a tiny dancer, presenter, author, mother, wife, daughter, sister and friend, my own canvas is decorated with beautiful experiences, memories and moments that have illuminated my life with joy and unexpected opportunities, creating a box that is painted in the unique shades of me. Over the years, I've embarked on a journey of self-discovery, exploring the vast expanse of who I am, and I've found a complex internal world that is teeming with myriad colours, talents and abilities. This wondrous adventure continues, an ongoing celebration of the richness within. And amid the whirlwind, that little girl who found joy in bananas paired with spaghetti remains an integral part of who I am. So, when faced with life's challenges, when the old adage suggests you should make lemonade from lemons, I propose a quirky twist: when life throws you lemons, switch it up and grab a banana. Embrace the unexpected, revel in·the thrill of the unconventional and savour the uniqueness that colours your journey. Life, much like your vibrantly adorned box, is a canvas waiting for your artistic touch.

'Be the light.'

UNKNOWN

CONCLUSION

THIS IS JUST THE BEGINNING ...

By writing a conclusion, this could seem like the end of your self-exploration journey. Because of this, I was very hesitant to write one to begin with. But the more I thought about it, the more I realised the importance of pausing in the midst of so many insights. It's easy to feel overwhelmed by new information, by the discoveries we've uncovered about ourselves on this journey. But taking a moment to look back, to pause and make space for new-found insights (not only into the workings of our minds and bodies, but also into our own essence) can be incredibly empowering.

Before you entertain any doubts about continuing your journey, it's important to say that there's no singular route that leads to self-discovery. This journey is intimate and deeply personal, tailored to your needs, preferences and rhythms. Just as some people thrive on five hours of sleep while others require eight, so, too, do we navigate our emotional landscapes in our own distinct ways. We are not all hardwired in the exact same way, and it's crucial you always remember this. In essence, this book isn't just about establishing routines or setting goals; it's a testament to you and the process you employ to uncover all the different parts of yourself. So, as you reach these final pages, remember this: you hold the key to unlocking a more fulfilled version of yourself, and the adventure of self-discovery is as vast and varied as you are.

So, as we wrap up our journey together, let's reflect on what we've explored – tapping into those four pillars that have been our guiding stars. You see, they're not just abstract concepts: they're friendly signposts along the path to understanding yourself and your unique rhythm in life. Imagine we've been on a road trip together. These four pillars serve as the trusty GPS that helps navigate us through the twists and turns of self-discovery. Sure, I've laid them out in a certain order throughout this book, but once you've got them, you can visit them at any time you like. Each chapter, each pillar, reveals its own gems of insight. And here's the beautiful part – there's no right or wrong way to use them. You might find yourself drawn to one pillar more than the others on certain days, and that's perfectly okay. It's all about finding what resonates with you. Remember those instances throughout when you paused to take a moment in order to really absorb what we discussed? Those are the moments that matter. Those are the whispers of your inner wisdom, nudging you towards a deeper understanding of yourself. And as you continue along your journey, those answers might change depending on the day, and that's not just okay – it's beautiful. We must never stop growing, and we must never stop being curious about ourselves and the world around us.

Let's briefly revisit each of these cornerstone elements – acceptance, reflection, the work and discovery – which play such a pivotal role in shaping how we perceive ourselves and the world around us.

ACCEPTANCE

In the chapters dedicated to acceptance, we explored the profound power of embracing ourselves exactly as we are: like stumbling upon a secret garden within us, lush with self-love that blossoms outward, enriching the lives of those around us. Understand that this self-love isn't just a feel-good notion. It lays the groundwork for unity, fostering deep connections with others. But acceptance merely opens the doors to a beautiful journey. As we immerse ourselves in love, we stumble upon something else: gratitude.

Through gratitude, we learn to appreciate the smallest blessings, finding solace and joy even within life's twists and turns. And the dance of gratitude leads us gracefully to kindness and forgiveness. Kindness is a language, a way of spreading light in a world that sometimes feels dim. And forgiveness? This is the ultimate elixir: a potent weapon against the darkness that creeps into our lives. But here's the twist – forgiveness and kindness aren't just for others. They're for ourselves, too. In forgiving ourselves, we release the heavy burdens of guilt and regret, making space for healing and growth. And in extending kindness to ourselves, we nourish the very essence of our being, fostering a sense of inner peace and self-compassion that knows no bounds.

REFLECTION

As we explored the chapters intertwined with the reflection pillar, we embarked on a profound journey of self-discovery, confronting the shadows that often lurk within us. These inner demons, the silent antagonists, emerged from the depths where we'd long attempted to evade them. Gazing into the mirror of our souls, we confronted those aspects of ourselves that we most avoided. The fear of failure, the fear of being a fraud, the fear of not being accepted – each a reflection of deeper complexities within us. But in acknowledging them, in embracing their presence, we gained a new-found strength. In facing them head-on, something incredible occurred – they lost their grip on us. In this dance of light and shadow, of virtue and vice, we discovered the exquisite beauty of human complexity. For it is in embracing both the light and the dark within us that we truly come to understand the essence of who we are. The good and the bad coming together ultimately showing us how together they are a key part to the beauty of being human.

THE WORK

Through this pillar, we explored the value of laying down foundations in order for effective transformation in our lives. Just like mastering dance steps one by one before showcasing a mesmerising performance, effecting change in our lives demands a similar approach. It's about embracing the process, taking those small, deliberate steps and gradually witnessing the transformation unfold. Through our discussions, we uncovered the profound magic hidden within the mundane. Yes, the seemingly ordinary routines and choices we make daily hold the power to yield extraordinary results in the long run. We recognised that there is beauty in the simplicity of our actions and began to understand that each tiny effort contributes to a larger, more meaningful outcome. We learned to celebrate the power of consistency and commitment – setting both big and small goals and relishing in the satisfaction of progress. Never forget that seemingly ordinary things can lead to extraordinary results. So, follow those routines, set those goals, and understand the importance of slowing down too, to listen to the voice inside yourself. Together, this creates the formula for change and gives you a beautiful sum: it gives you results.

DISCOVERY

The most wondrous part of learning more about who we are is all the new discoveries that come along with it. Throughout the chapters dedicated to discovery, we embarked on the captivating adventure of revelation. With each layer we peeled back, we stumbled upon hidden treasures within ourselves – aspects and nuances we may have overlooked or forgotten, perhaps even since the days of our childhood. Rekindling the flame of our inner child allows us to once again open our hearts and minds to see things through a broader lens. Suddenly, our perspective widens, allowing us to view the world through a kaleidoscope of creativity and inspiration, enriching every facet of our existence, be it personal or professional. Discovery also allows us to take a step back and take notice of the possessions we may have deemed a source or cause of happiness, and understand that they may not necessarily be as high in value as we once believed. Discovery helps us to realise that true happiness often lies in the simplest of things. Whether it be the warmth of genuine connections, in the laughter shared with loved ones or in embracing the richness. of what truly matters to us. The pillar of discovery is one filled with colour and wonder, acting as a reminder to break free from the constraints of convention and embrace the magic hidden within the unexpected. So, next time life hands you lemons, why not reach for a banana instead? After all, it's by allowing yourself to think outside the box that you stumble upon life's sweets surprises.

FEAR: **F**LIP **E**VERY **A**NXIOUS **R**EACTION

One word mentioned consistently throughout this book was fear. Fear can take control of our lives: fear of the unknown, fear of ourselves, fear of the future. Through the centuries, fear has gone from being our protector in a world where we fought for survival on a daily basis to now becoming the one thing that stops our growth more than anything else. It can be the emotion that takes centre stage in our daily decisions, preventing us from experiencing, learning and growing as a community. If we learn to recognise fear for what it is, we may, perhaps, make better choices: in how we react to things, or how we allow new experiences in. It's crucial for me to remind you that fear really does come in all shapes and sizes and can very sneakily hide in those small crevices within us. The fear that many of us feel and must constantly combat with our own light is the fear of not being enough.

You are enough! We all are. You just need to allow your-self to see it.

And yet these are the words that my dear and late friend Robin Windsor never believed for himself.

As I reflect on the personal journey of my friend I am struck by the profound impact that fear can wield over our lives. Robin and I shared an incredible bond for over eleven years. He was the very first person I met when I joined the cast of *Burn the Floor*. He welcomed me with his bright blue eyes, gorgeous smile and infectious personality. Robin was a true force of nature, gracing Broadway, the West End and other stages across the globe, and dazzling millions of people every week with his incredible talent during his time on *Strictly Come Dancing*. And his achievements were not confined to the stage. He also dedicated himself to charitable endeavours, particularly those focused on mental-health awareness. He always aimed to create a safe space where everyone's thoughts and emotions could not only be shared, but also truly be heard. Despite his boundless generosity and genuine kindness, Robin constantly battled with a relentless fear; a shadow that seemed to follow him, looming over all the beautiful facets that encompassed his being. He never quite felt like he was enough, and as someone who knew him and knew how untrue that was, knowing that he could never see himself the way others saw him will always be one of the hardest things for me to sit with personally. The dimming of his bright light is a loss that will forever weigh heavy on me. Yet, in his absence, I hope Robin can serve as a reminder of the inherent beauty and strength within each of us. That his light, although a little farther away, continues to shine as a beacon of hope; hope that we embrace our own light and let it shine while we remain fortunate enough to have the time to do so. I implore you to confront fear with unwavering resolve because within you lies a reservoir of untapped potential. Embrace the fullness of your being, and allow your light to shine unapologetically, for it is and will always be more than enough.

It's true that fear wears many disguises, often lurking in the smallest corners of our being. However, amidst the shadows, there shines brightly an everlasting beacon of truth no one can ever take away from you – YOU ARE ENOUGH.

A POWERFUL TOOL

The most powerful tool – more powerful than anything I may have shared with you in this book – is your desire to want to find more of the wonder that is you. You are the most powerful being in this world, and this book is only just flipping on the light switch that ignites you. I urge you to continue to learn, to grow, to discover, to unleash, to work towards feeding that light that exists within you more and more every day. It's the biggest gift that you can give not just to yourself, but to the world. If we all desired to expand this beam of magic that lives within us, the world as we know it would be completely different. It may sound like a childish fantasy to say that one person can make a difference; that one person can help make the world a better place. But as we discovered, we need to tap into our innocent and child-like thoughts more; remove the cynic that fights the joy of the child within us. Like when we were children, continue being optimistic, believe that the 'good guy' will always win, and that love and kindness are the strongest weapons we can ever yield in this world.

I am deeply grateful that you chose to pick up this book, but mostly, I'm grateful that you were brave enough to reflect on the parts of yourself that were yearning to be accepted and explored. As a mother now, I hope that with each small step I take in this life, and with every person I encounter – whether through this book or some other means – I am helping to reflect the light that beams from each of us. In turn, I hope this will help to lay a foundation of acceptance and joy for the future world that Lyra will grow up in. Please have the courage to keep exploring and questioning – with an open mind and an open heart – the big world within you, so that collectively we can begin to face the wider world with more kindness and confidence. Whether it's pursuing your dreams by taking small, steady steps, reaching out to that friend in need or indulging in spontaneous dance classes, let's cultivate a community that supports our mutual growth. Remember, in the mosaic of life, every shape and colour – the good, the bad and the imperfect – contributes to the beauty of the whole. Do not let fear be your guide; instead, believe in hope and have faith in the good that exists in us all. Live courageously, and above all … be the light.

I'll leave you with this poem by Rumi:

THE GUEST HOUSE

This being human is a guest house.
Every morning a new arrival.

A joy, a depression, a meanness,
some momentary awareness comes
as an unexpected visitor.

Welcome and entertain them all!
Even if they're a crowd of sorrows,
who violently sweep your house
empty of its furniture,
still, treat each guest honourably.
He may be clearing you out
for some new delight.

The dark thought, the shame, the malice,
meet them at the door laughing,
and invite them in.

Be grateful for whoever comes,
because each has been sent
as a guide from beyond.

ACKNOWLEDGEMENTS

Thank you to my agents at Curtis Brown and Milk Management for always believing me, with a special mention to Gordon Wise for helping make this book become a reality.

Thank you to William Collins for giving me this wonderful opportunity to share this book with everyone, especially to Bengono Bessala, who believed in it from day one, and Hazel Eriksson, who were with me, guiding me every step of the way. I could not have done it without you.

Thank you to Halestorm PR for helping me be seen authentically.

Thank you to my dance teachers, Manuel and Lory Castro, Jason Gilkison and Peta Roby, and all of my *Burn the Floor* family. You have shaped my life and career immensely. You exude your passion for the art of dance in all that you do.

Thank you to the BBC for bringing me to the UK and allowing it to be my new home.

Thank you to my tribe of friends who have become my family away from family.

My deepest thank you to my family, who are my rock, my constants, my light in this world! My husband, Aljaž. My parents, Maritza and Luis. My brother, Alejandro, and with a special mention to my co-writer and little sister, Lesly Marie. Thank you for doing this with me. You are a talent beyond your years. I love you all more than you can ever imagine.

And to my biggest inspiration in life, my daughter, Lyra Rose. Thank you for giving me purpose and meaning to continue forever moving forward. May you grow up in a world that will allow your light to always shine bright. I love you with all my heart and soul.

RESOURCES

If you need to talk, any time of day or night, these free listening services offer confidential support from trained volunteers. You can talk about anything that's troubling you, no matter how difficult:

SAMARITANS

Call 116 123 to talk to Samaritans, or
    email jo@samaritans.org
https://www.samaritans.org/how-we-can-help/
    contact-samaritan/

CRISIS TEXT LINE

Text SHOUT to 85258 to contact the Shout Crisis Text
Line, or text YM if you're under 19. They give
confidential support 24/7 via text.
https://www.crisistextline.uk/

CHILDLINE

If you're under 19, you can call 0800 1111 to talk to
Childline. The number will not appear on your
phone bill.
https://www.childline.org.uk/

NHS SERVICES

The NHS offers both emergency assistance and can also
arrange referrals for counselling and other therapeutic
services.
https://www.nhs.uk/nhs-services/mental-health-services/

REFERENCES

1. Tiffany Sauber Millacci, 'What Is Gratitude and Why Is It So Important?', PositivePsychology.com (28 February 2017): https://positivepsychology.com/gratitude-appreciation/ ?utm_content=cmp-true

2. 'Why Giving Makes You Feel so Good', Ramsey Solutions (26 August 2021): https://www.ramseysolutions.com/budgeting/ why-giving-makes-you-feel-good

3. American Psychological Association, 'In Rich and Poor Nations, Giving Makes People Feel Better Than Getting, Research Finds', press release (21 February 2013): https://www.apa.org/news/press/releases/2013/02/ people-giving

4. Lara B. Aknin et al., 'Prosocial Spending and Well-being: Cross-cultural Evidence for a Psychological Universal', *Journal of Personality and Social Psychology* (2013), Vol. 104, No. 4, 635–52

5. Kirtika Surolia, 'Fear Has Two Meanings – Choice is Yours', TheMindFool (22 April 2020): https://themindfool.com/ fear-has-two-meanings/

6. P. R. Clance & S. A. Imes, 'The Imposter Phenomenon in High Achieving Women: Dynamics and Therapeutic Intervention', *Psychotherapy: Theory, Research & Practice* (1978), Vol. 15, No. 3, 241–247

7. Amal Saymeh, 'What is Imposter Syndrome? Definition, Symptoms, and Overcoming It', BetterUp (22 February 2023): https://www.betterup.com/blog/what-is-imposter-syndrome-and-how-to-avoid-it

8. Gabriele Oettingen, *Rethinking Positive Thinking: Inside the New Science of Motivation* (London, Penguin Publishing Group), 2015

9. Philip Brickman and Donald Campbell, 'Hedonic Relativism and Planning the Good Society' (1971), in M. H. Appley (Ed.), *Adaptation-level Theory: A Symposium* (New York, Academic Press), 287–305

10. Charles Duhigg, *The Power of Habit: Why We Do What We Do, and How to Change* (London, Penguin Random House), 2013

11. Phillippa Lally, Cornelia H. M. van Jaarsveld, Henry W. W. Potts and Jane Wardle, 'How Are Habits Formed: Modelling Habit Formation in the Real World', *European Journal of Social Psychology* (2009), Vol. 40, Issue 6, 998–1009

12. Corey Keyes, *Languishing: How to Feel Alive in a World That Wears Us Down* (London, Crown Publishing), 2024

13. Corey Keyes and Jonathan Haidt, *Flourishing: Positive Psychology and the Life Well Lived* (Washington, DC, American Psychological Association), 2002

14. A. H. Maslow, 'A Theory of Human Motivation', *Psychological Review* (1943), Vol. 50, Issue 4, 370–396

15. Philip Brickman and Donald Campbell, 'Hedonic Relativism and Planning the Good Society' (1971), in M. H. Appley

(Ed.), *Adaptation-level Theory: A Symposium* (New York, Academic Press), 287–305.

16. Fred B. Bryant and Joseph Veroff, *Savouring: A New Model of Positive Experience* (Oxford, Routledge), 2006

17. Daniela Ramirez-Duran, 'Savoring in Positive Psychology: 21 Tools to Appreciate Life', PositivePsychology.com (5 February 2021): https://positivepsychology.com/savoring/